Grandma's Pudding

And Other Stories of a Ripley Miner

T0347154

Grandma's Pudding

And Other Stories of a Ripley Miner

Keith Staley

The
History
Press

Frontispiece: Keith Staley, 1954.

First published 2007
Reprinted 2020

The History Press,
97 St George's Place, Cheltenham,
Gloucestershire, GL50 3QB
www.tempus-publishing.com

Tempus Publishing is an imprint of NPI Media Group

British Library Cataloguing in Publication Data.
A catalogue record for this book is available from the British Library.

ISBN 978 0 7524 4483 3

Typesetting and origination by NPI Media Group
Printed in Great Britain by TJ International Ltd, Padstow, Cornwall.

Grandma's Pudding

A Lad's Dream Come True

There's something quite fascinating about a ride on the footplate of an engine; most people all their lives want to have such an experience. I was very lucky, as my dad, 'bless him', was able to allow me that privilege. My dad was a boilersmith, and his job was to look after the huge Lancashire boilers at all the collieries belonging to the Butterley Company. This job was a family concern, as three generations of the Staley family had been the entire staff of the company. As boilersmiths, they were responsible for the smooth running of the coal mines in Derbyshire, and to some extent in Nottinghamshire.

Another side of the job was the retubing of the engine's boilers, locos we called them. These steam locos pulled the wagons full of coal, the life blood of the mines, backwards and forwards to the factories and iron foundries in and around the district. Retubing had to be done when the tubes were leaking, an amazing array of long pipes inside the body of the engine. Filled with water, they would be heated up with the glowing fire in the fire box.

One of the main runs, as I remember, was from Brittain Colliery to Ripley Colliery, and then on to Marehay, over the main Ripley/Derby line to Derby. It was a wonderful sight to see wagonloads of hard-won coal going on its way, bringing prosperity to our town of Ripley.

On this particular day – I think it was a Saturday – I was down at Brittain Colliery down by the police headquarters. My mother had asked me to take dad some sandwiches and a bottle of tea, as he had to wait for the boiler inspector to examine the W.D. loco dad and his mate had been working on. Being Saturday afternoon only a handful of men were at work, so it was quite easy to go into the pit yard without anyone asking me what my business was. I remember making my way round the back of the screens and making a beeline for the loco shed. Just as a matter of interest, the screens are where the coal is sorted from the dirt, and graded, from small cobbles up to the big lumps we used to get delivered by horse and cart once a month.

Dad greeted me with a smile, and introduced me to his mate Bill, and the inspector. 'What do you think of this then?' said the inspector, rubbing his hands on some cotton waste to clean them. I stood there taking it all in, admiring this great beast, wheels almost as tall as me. I just wondered what it would be like up there on the footplate. I looked at dad, full of pride, my dad, yes it was my dad who had repaired the loco, and now stood waiting for the inspector to pass it fit for duty.

'Right Les! I'm off', said the inspector, striding off towards a car I could see was almost new. It was a Rover, about a 1945 model, shining in the afternoon sun, black and silver, with a marvellous chrome radiator, and spoked wire wheels. '

Okay then,' said dad, 'we had better get a fire going in the old girl,' climbing up the steps and gripping the hand rail to pull himself into the cab. Opening the double fire-box door, two halves that is, he proceeded to stuff in paper, old oily rags and a great bundle of firewood. Looking round for Bill, he said, 'chuck us a match,' in a broad Derbyshire accent, and lit the fire.

Ivor Staley, step-brother of Leslie.

The fire was soon blazing away, and with the coal added it soon put on some steam. I watched the needle as it slowly crept round, and a bubble was dancing in a glass tube, water surging up and down, this showing the amount of water we had in the tanks.

In what seemed a very short time, steam was up, and dad asked Bill if he would fetch Fred over, as he was the loco driver, only he was authorised to move the loco. While Bill had gone over to get Fred the driver, dad took my hand, and pulled me up into the cab. 'Now then, me lad,' dad said, looking at me with a twinkle in his eye, 'keep o'wt of the road when Fred comes, stand well back from the fire and you'll be alright'. With that, he opened the fire-box doors and shovelled more coal onto the fire.

'What's that dad'? I said, looking at a chain hanging down. At the end of the chain was an oval ring, big enough to get three fingers in. 'Give me your hand and I'll show you,' he said, lifting me up. 'Pull down, gently and let go when I tell you,' dad said. There was an almighty blast, as the whistle wailed out on full song. Talk about being frightened to death, I let that chain go as though I'd been electrocuted!

'Pressure's up!' said dad, as Bill and Fred came sauntering along, each with a woodbine in the corner of his mouth. 'Right, up you get', said Fred, 'and stand clear of the fire doors'.

With a terrific blast on the whistle, we gently eased our way across the points, and onto the line that would take us out by the screens, heading in the direction of Ripley pit. There was some water on the rails, and as we set off, the wheels of the engine spun in a surge of power as the wheels tried hard to grip the greasy surface.

At last we were on our way, speed picking up, as the steam pressure increased, and the air bubble danced merrily in the glass tube above the fire box. That sound, only heard on railways, was a joy to hear, clickerty click, clickerty click, as we passed over the joints in the rails. Holding on tight to the hand rail, I was told to look out. Ahead of us was a sweeping bend in the track, and Fred had to slow the engine down with the regulator handle, as we negotiated the bend.

All along the track side, you could see rabbits scurrying about, diving in their burrows as if they had been shot at. It was a sunny day, and as we made our way along the track, the air was a cloud of white billowing down, coming from the tall wild flowers growing either side on the banks. A sparrow hawk was high in the sky, hovering silently, looking for a tasty meal. Suddenly it dived, and to my amazement, caught a field mouse and killed it with one grab of its sharp beak. This was not only a train ride, but also a nature study.

Meanwhile, Bill had opened his haversack, the contents spread all over the top of a tool box. Unwrapping the paper, he revealed some fatty bacon, and proceeded to cut off the rind with his knife. Fred, on seeing the bacon, opened the fire-box door and pushed in the long narrow shovel, with which the fire was kept going with coal.

'What are you doing?' I inquired. 'I'm cleaning the shovel, ready for the bacon,' he said. 'You've never tasted bacon, till you've had it off the shovel.' Out came the shovel, almost red hot, and Bill dropped the bacon on. Hot fat spat out as the fire doors were opened and the shovel held in the glowing fire. Within seconds, it was done and placed on to thick slices of homemade bread.

'Get that down yer!' Bill, grease dripping off his chin, had almost finished before I had started, and dad just stood and laughed. Well, what can one say! Never in my life have I enjoyed bacon so much, fatty or not. 'Only killed last week,' said Bill, 'a bit of all right.' It appears he had a bit of a smallholding, a couple of pigs, and about a dozen fowls.

Anyway, by this time we were getting very near to the Iron Bridge: this was a bridge over the main road from Ripley to Nottingham. 'Keep him out of sight,' said Fred to my dad, as we rolled and rattled over the bridge, the bridge letting out all sorts of groans as we passed over. I couldn't see, but I could hear the trolley bus go beneath us, the pulleys crackling as power left the overhead wires and travelled down the long poles into the motor of the trolley.

Patches had formed in the bank where sparks had fallen sometime from the loco and set off grass fires. That was one of the hazards of the old steam engine, always the chance of a fire, especially if we had a decent summer. 'Right my lad, this is where you get off,' said dad, looking straight at me. 'Your time's up, I don't think you've had a bad day; your mother will be worrying.' 'Oh dad, just a bit longer,' I said with a long face. The loco slowed: we were getting near Ripley pit. 'Say thank you to Bill and Fred,' said dad, as he lowered me down the steps. Reaching the floor and looking up, steam obstructing my view for a second, I said my farewells and scrambled through a hole in the hedge bottom; a hole I had gone through many times before.

The loco was put in reverse, and with a cloud of steam engulfing both engine and men, I made my way home, a matter of a few yards. What a day, I couldn't get to school fast enough the following Monday to tell my friends about my dad and his W.D. locomotive. This is a true story.

Dreaming - 1926

The world outside, we were not aware!
Politicians, promises, no work, despair.

Men picking coal, on tips of spoil,
Taking in washing, a woman's toil.

Women wailing, babies crying,
No National Health, for even the dying.

'Players and woodbines! twopence a packet,
Collection for the Doctor, what a racket.

Best suit for Sunday… was all we had.
Cast-offs for school, for which we were glad.

Hob-nailed boots, patches galore,
Standing on street corners… what a bore!

The *Daily Herald* was our paper then,
Dreams of tomorrow… a golden horizon when?

Trams on the streets, … oh! what a ride,
'Long Live the King,' we sang it with pride.

Grandma's Pudding

As a boy of the small mining village of Waingroves, I made it one of my duties that most Sundays I would call at grandma's for dinner and do any errands that wanted doing.

As I walked in at the back door, she would be at the sink, a large stone washbasin, worn away by time and the years of pit clothes being washed in it. Bent over with age and hard work, she would be scraping the new potatoes, taken out of the large garden most mining cottages seemed to have – something left over from a bygone era.

I was always greeted with a smile, and she would say to me, with a twinkle in her eyes, 'What you come for?' Knowing full well the reason. Anyway, on going in, the first thing to catch my eye would be a jug, a jug with a large chip in the rim.

This jug was placed on the table, to one side of the vegetables, ready for me to nip over to the 'beer off' across the road. Naturally after many such journeys, I began to acquire a taste for Mansfield Bitter. Putting the potatoes in an old iron saucepan – one of a set of three – she would poke the fire, 'a collier's coal fire', and then arrange the cobbles around the hob, on to which the saucepan was placed.

Once the potatoes were out of the way, grandma produced a board out of a large pantry, on which we were to mix a pudding masterpiece. Out came the Co-op flour, the block of lard, a bottle of milk, half a cup of water, and last of all, a Denby pottery earthenware mixing bowl.

The table top was covered, as most other working-class tables were covered, in oil-cloth. Opening the bag of flour, she would shake it until there was a good three inches in the bowl. Reaching for the lard, lumps would be cut off the half-pound block with a knife that had visited the kitchen step many, many times for sharpening.

Placing her hands, 'gnarled with years of scrubbing floors', into the bowl, she would knead the flour and lard together, squeezing and pummelling, until most of the lumps had disappeared. It was a sort of dough, and this was rolled out, on to the board, like a deflated football. grandma seemed quite oblivious of the odd splinter.

'Come on,' she would say, 'wash your hands and you can spread the jam'. 'Can we have raspberry?' I would say, as that was my favourite. When I had covered the surface, perhaps using as much as a third of the jam, I would lick my fingers, jam all around my mouth.

The watered-down milk would be brushed around the edges of the pudding. Once this was done, this overgrown pancake, this soggy dumpling, was rolled up – loosely of course, otherwise the jam would be lost. From a drawer, grandma would get an old tea towel that had known better days. The pudding, placed on the cloth, would be wrapped up, and tied with string, acquired from the parcel of groceries delivered every Saturday morning by a man and boy and one of those wonderful Co-op lorries with a low back for easy loading, and a wooden beam down the centre, about 4ft 6in from the lorry floor. This beam, plus a tarpaulin, was cover for the goods in inclement weather.

To get back to the pudding, which by this time looked ready for the post office, another iron saucepan, black as the ace of spades, was taken down from a nail driven into the kitchen wall.

Half filling the pan with water, the pudding was placed in the fire, to boil, and then simmer for what seemed ages. Adding water to keep a constant level was another duty I took on whilst the table was set. The table would be set for three, grandad sitting in pride of place near the fire.

On the dot, 12.30 p.m. to be precise, the meat, 'the Sunday joint', would be placed just left of grandad's place. By the way, in order to get his baccy and pint, he would perhaps have swept a couple of chimneys in the village, long before I was out of bed. The dinner was… different from mother's, to say the least, with its watery gravy, but how I enjoyed it.

Lifting the scalding pudding out of the saucepan was a work of art: fishing for it, with a huge meat fork, the handle solid bone, yellowed with age. Eventually the roly-poly pudding was unwrapped and cut up into generous helpings. Custard was taboo; milk served straight from the bottle was best. The milk would be poured on the pudding and there would be an instant ring of fat on top of the milk.

Eating the pudding scalding hot was the secret of enjoyment – in fact, the jam used to burn my tongue. There was one thing to be said for a portion of this fantastic pudding – it was filling, the first spoonful would warn your stomach of things to come.

Those Sunday dinners with my grandparents, memories of my childhood, will remain with me forever. A true story.

Grandad and Ivor's mother – second wife to grandad – on a day's outing in Skegness.

Mill Hill School pathway – Ripley pit to Waingroves.

Railway line to Brittain pit.

Snooker hall, Ripley.

Hills beer-off, Waingroves.

Rowbothams chip-shop bus terminus, Beighton Street, Ripley.

He Giveth, He Taketh

Oh what sadness,
Oh the joy.
God in heaven.
The gift… a boy.

Not long to live,
I know not why.
Angels surround him
'To have', and then give.

For a while he was mine,
To have and to hold.
I kneel by his grave,
My story to unfold.

Praise be to God,
There's room I'll be bound,
My boy in heaven.

Angelic music, a chorus, the sound.
Hallelujah praise the Lord,
The highest on high,
Almighty… Adored.

Spring in Derbyshire

It's almost May, the blossoms out
The daffodils in their brilliance shout,
Hedgerows turn green as the buds appear,
The fields turned over, the sky so clear,

Newborn lambs, the daisies on display,
Fresh green grass, and then to our dismay,

Snow… Like cotton wool floating down,
Blankets the fields with its own gown,

The birds hide from the wintry blast,
With Heavens so white, so overcast,

The daffodils bend as if to say,
How did this happen? A bright spring day.

Codnor and Scrambled Eggs

It was a hot clammy night, July 1948, I remember as if it were yesterday. The suit I was wearing was brand new (in those days, navy blue was the rage), a white shirt with long pointed collar, a silver tie and black patent shoes, pointed toes of course.

I had read in the local paper that a dance was on at the local Miners' Welfare and as I had just passed my exam for ballroom dancing, I was on the prowl. 'Ladies watch out,' I thought as I slapped on the 'Dennis Compton' Brylcreem, sliced out a parting in my hair, and slipped £1 8s into my trouser pocket.

Twenty-eight shillings was my week's wages from the colliery at the bottom of our street. Sweat beads appeared on my brow as I set off to the Welfare. To tell the truth, I had always been a bit of a loner. Not with the girls, of course, but men friends and boozing didn't interest me at all. Work and dancing took up all my time.

On arriving at the dance, I paid my two shillings, got my free raffle ticket and stood in a corner near the four-piece band. The band was blasting out a jive number and the floor was filled with couples twisting and turning, the young ladies' knickers in full view as the short flared skirts spun around their waists and their hair flew all over the place.

I stood and waited for the waltz and quickstep to be announced, the microphone whining from time to time as the drummer knocked back a quick half pint and splashed down the microphone; the next dance please. After the jive, most of the couples were glad to sit the next dance out, so seeing my chance for a bit of cheek to cheek, I made for this slip of a girl that I had been watching: she had sat through the jiving sipping a shandy with ice.

My approach was always well mannered: none of this, 'Do you wonna dance' lark with me, it wasn't always the rough approach that paid off. I knew her slightly and she smiled as she put down the shandy and we took the floor. We were the first on the floor, the lights were lowered and the waltz began. I led her on to the floor and that instant we were as one. My right arm was round her waist, pulling her to me, my left hand softly holding her right hand, damp with sweat, about head high. The waltz was dreamy, and as we danced I looked into her eyes and could see my reflection.

Cup final outing. From left to right: Keith Staley, - ? -, Leslie Staley, Ivor Staley 'Jun'.

Keith Staley, Holes Moor Farm, scrambling.

My height is 5ft 8in, and her head fit snug on my chest as we swirled around the dance floor, quite oblivious of anyone or anything.

We seemed to take an instant liking to each other and we paused, suddenly realising the tempo had changed to a quickstep. She laughed as we bumped a couple who had decided we had had the floor to ourselves long enough. The music stopped: we stood for a second or two and then I was tapped on the shoulder by the M.C. of the dance, who, with a beaming smile, presented me with this wicker basket. Inside were three dozen new-laid eggs: low and behold, we had won the spot prize!

Above our heads was a glittering revolving ball. I thanked the MC amidst applause, and we made our way back to the young lady's table. Well! 'What about that then?' I said, putting the basket under the table, 'You have brought me luck.' I saw her lips move to reply and that instant was knocked off my seat and right through some French windows.

I later found out it was a drunken lout that had overbalanced and pushed me. There was broken glass all over the floor and my arm was bleeding through a rip in my new suit. I was flat on my back and the young woman was screaming as she leaned over me. I felt this sticky sensation and I thought, 'God, my hands are cut.' It wasn't blood, though – three dozen eggs were scrambled. I was plastered in slimy raw egg and my arm was bleeding quite heavily. The youth was thrown out: everyone full of apologies, I was helped to my feet and the young lady and I escorted to a car someone had brought round.

Green Grass and Memories

There's a field nearby, and on a summer's night, when all is still, and windows are open wide, and you listen very hard… you can hear the sounds of bygone days.

There's the blower, the old ship's fog horn calling men and boys to work. 'A whooshing,' a noise that can only come from the huge steam winding engine, lowering the night shift gently into the bowels of the earth.

A humming sound filters over on the night air: the power house, in all its glory. Red paint, gold paint, dark green, it's all there if you close your eyes. Birds chirping in the eaves, the singing of a kettle and the fizz as it boils over onto the fire bars.

Turn over, restless, it's there again! The buzz of a circular wood saw, you open the large double doors – watch out! A great big belt is driving the saw from a motor covered in grime and newly cut sawdust. The sawyer puts up his hand to wave; two fingers of the left hand are down to the first joint. 'Shut that blasted door,' he shouts, sawdust billowing in great clouds.

You sit up in bed! Am I hearing things? Clang, clang goes his hammer, the blacksmith shaping a shoe for that marvellous Shire horse standing so proud.

'Come on owd lad, lift thee foot up.' Into the glowing fire go the tongs, and out comes a partly made shoe, bits shooting off, the scale lightly tapped off on the anvil, then gently lowered onto the great beast's hoof.

Straight away, into your nostrils comes the smell of burning hoof. A smell, nothing in the world like it; memories, sweet, sweet memories. The blacksmith and his mate the striker, sweat teeming off them, a picture so vivid in one's mind.

There's a 'toot toot' as the loco shunts the empty wagons under the screens, 'no such thing as washery plants in those days'. A shuffling sound, a cloud of black dust as the conveyor is lowered into the wagons, delivering hard-won coal, the wealth of this county of ours. To add to this! This source of energy unleashed, of men, and machines!

A bell rings out! The 'whooshing' sound takes over; huge steel cages dangling on threads of steel lock-coiled ropes are passing in the shaft as water cascades onto men 'black as the night,' finding its way between brickwork to fall 450 yards into the pit bottom.

Some would say I was dreaming on this summer night, but you see, this field was my playground as a child, my livelihood as a man. Do you believe in ghosts?

Music While You Work

The year was 1941, and I was a child of nine years of age, living through the hell of wartime, a shortage of sweets, clothes and very little spending money. In those days, there was no television or videos and we had to make our own entertainment as times were very hard.

I suppose as a family we were lucky, in as much dad had full-time employment at the pit, and my eldest sister was employed full time as a machinist with I.R. Morley's of Heanor, a large factory that produced nylon stockings and all types of knitwear.

The treat of the week was to go to the pictures, usually a war film with the Americans winning the war. Extra on the show would be the Pathé News, a very depressing account of how we were countering the German army in Europe, and the bombing of London and Coventry, the devastation and death. It was not a pretty sight for children, I still remember, and in a way I'm glad I was able to witness those films.

Getting the ninepence in old money to go to the pictures was a work of art; if dad was out at work or on duty as an air-raid warden I waited until my eldest sister's young man came round: when he was sitting in the front room, I would pounce. It wouldn't be many minutes before the young man had his hand in his pocket and gently edged me towards the door, a loud 'clear off' in my ear as I closed the door of the front room and made my way into the kitchen to put a bit of polish on my shoes before setting off. If when I arrived at the pictures it was an 'A' film, I had to wait for a couple to go in to get my ticket, as you had to be with an adult.

Those nights I stayed in, I shall never forget… my sister and her friends making their ballroom dresses on mum's Singer sewing machine. Clothing coupons were like gold then, so the girls had to do the best they could with any material at hand. There were Joan and Joyce, both about the same age as my sister – a team that in a couple of nights could knock together a long ballroom dress any large store would be proud to have on display in the window. Then, there was dancing, a man and woman with the width of a bus ticket between them as they danced the waltz and the quickstep to bands such as Victor Sylvestor, Geraldo, Ted Heath, Oscar Rabin, and the one and only Joe Loss. Sometimes I used to sneak off to the local drill hall, and watch for a chance to dance with the local girls.

Of course we had our share of Americans, both black and white, some very home sick, and often there would be a fight, with the military police having to intervene. I got on with all of them: a smile was enough to get a bar of chocolate or some chewing gum.

It was my job at weekends to ask one or two of them to tea: my mother always put on a smashing tea with whatever we had, and made them welcome. My grandmother, bless her, had a German upright piano in the parlour, a Beckstein if I remember correctly after all these years, a piano with a marvellous tone. Sometimes at the weekend the whole family would visit and take along one of the young men I had picked out of the hundreds stationed in our town. One soldier we took with us could make that piano talk: it gave my grandparents immense pleasure to sit and listen, and I feel very sad now when I think some of those lads never came back from the war. My collection of cap badges from the different regiments grew and grew as we befriended those sons of mothers living in different parts of the country. God bless them.

The war carried on and as time passed, my thoughts were not of going out to play with my pals – you couldn't, what with the black-outs and the bombing, all you could think of was getting to bed early in case we had an air raid. I remember when the siren sounded, mam would

Midland General bus, A7.

Above: My mother, Gertrude Elizabeth Eddie Johnstone – present at the scuttling of the *Graff-Spey* battleship. Moreley's answer to the war effort.

Opposite: My beloved sister, Kathleen Olga Staley, at eighteen.

take me downstairs to the bathroom and place me in the bath, wrapped in blankets just in case a bomb dropped on us. I suppose no one ever thought about the hot-water tank over my head and the scalding water.

These were the instructions given out on the radio on how to take cover if there wasn't a shelter nearby: many's the time I've laid in the bath listening to Tommy Handley and ITMA! With 'Fumf' and 'Can I do you now, Sir!' Sunday nights with Albert Sandler and the Palm Court Orchestra... Charlie Chester, Tommy Trinder doing their best to make us laugh. *Workers' Playtime*, and *Music While You Work* were very popular programmes in the 1940s, the BBC trying their utmost to bring some cheer to the British people in a time of confusion and frustration, not knowing what the next few hours or the night would bring.

Arthur Askey, Derek Roy and Frankie Howard had us in stitches with their jokes: jokes about the food rationing, the black market, Herr Schickelgruber – Adolf Hitler, as he was known– and the marvellous Bud Flannegan with his rendering of 'Underneath the Arches'.

I was on my way to school one summer's day, passing by the market place, and noticed a crowd of people standing around a German plane that had been shot down and was going from town to town on show. The man in charge had a loud-hailer in his hand, and was exhorting the crowd to press forward and take a look at the enemy plane.

'Three pence to sit in the cockpit, that's all ladies and gentlemen, step right up…' In my pocket was a threepenny bit for my milk and biscuits at break time but today no one would prize that threepenny bit from my hand: I had every intention of sitting in that cockpit seat and savouring those few moments of fantasy. At 4 p.m. the bell was rung and I raced to get my coat: I meant to be first in line for the German plane. There were wooden steps up to the cockpit, and I took them two at a time, feeling in my pocket for my money. The man held out his hand, and I'll never forget it – I searched and searched for that threepenny bit, but it was GONE! Tears flooded my face: it was too much to bear. 'Come on me lad, tha'll hay to goo, that holdin up tuthers,' the man said. 'Can I just sit a minute please?' I said, spragging myself against the steps. 'No money, so hop it!' the man said, and I had to go home, crying all the way. Mr Marsden was his name, burned on my mind to this day. We pass in the street today without a glance – he doesn't remember me of course – but I can assure you I will always remember the meanest man of our town at that time. Tea time and supper time I was still crying, the pillow wet as I lay in bed wishing all sorts of things on that man.

Many things came to try us during those terrible war days, like cows getting blown up at Langley Mill, the planes offloading their bombs after missing the bombing run on Rolls Royce's factory a few miles away.

During daylight, our own big heavy bombers used to come over the town doing practice runs on Lady Bower Dam, ready for the strike at the huge dams in the Ruhr Valley of Germany, the dams that produced the power for the German war effort. Barnes Wallis, the inventor of the Bouncing Bomb that destroyed those dams in Germany, was born in our town of Ripley. I can just imagine him listening to *Music While You Work* while he was studying the flight of the bomb over the surface of the water.

Ripley at War!

Butterley company, glory and all,
Work for the masses, that was the call.
St Pancras in London, building bridges galore.
Pride in our work, backs aching and sore.

Cast-iron arches, reaching up to the sky,
The year of '39, war drawing nigh.
Butterley Company, Barnes Wallis, the bomb.
In our time of need – was help to come?

School railings disappeared, we needed the steel,
Gas masks were issued, 'Bells' no longer peeled.
'Tighten your belts', was asked of the nation.
Guns, in place of cars, what a situation!

War-bonds were sold, to bring in the money,
Flag days were held, it pays to be ready.
U-boats abound, all around our shores,
Food and clothing was short, as were the toys.

Long the night, as the sirens sounded,
Fog all around, our fighter planes grounded.
Deep in our shelters, away from the blast,
Praying through the night, the dawn – arriving at last.

Churchill appeals, to the commonwealth he broadcast.
We need your help! Let words not be wasted,
Rally round… and together we'll win.
Together, through France to where it began.
Wellington bombers, Lancasters, Spitfires too,
Parts made in Derby, for the 'first of the few'.
Those brave lads, so gallant, so brave,
Gave back this country, for our children to save.

Ripley today, as Ripley was then,
Not much has changed, since the war began,
Butterley has gone; we now have a bypass,
The town hall's still with us, fresh paint, new glass.

Gone, the flax factory, coal mines and all,
Memories are all that remain, of the war, and the toil.
Ripley I know – the Ripley I love,
In this town, I was born, with help from above.

The Red Bike

During my school days, I had the unfortunate experience of having my cycle stolen. That cycle was my most treasured possession, as my dad had given it to me after years of pressure for him to buy me one. Father's bike was a Raleigh 'Speed King', with a Sturmey Archer three speed, and I loved that bike more than any other thing I possessed. Black and chrome, it shone like new as I polished it with loving care, not wanting to go out in the rain when asked to run errands.

Anyway, the fateful day came when my bike was stolen. My world ended that instant; tears were shed by the bucketful. The police were informed, but I really didn't care: my bike was gone and I was heartbroken. Friday was the day of the theft, and I will never forget that dreadful day at school. Always one of the first out of class, I made my way to the cycle stands, my pump in my hand. The bike was placed in the same stand almost every day, but to my horror the stand was empty. I went through every stand one by one there was no Raleigh three-speeder. Tears began to swell in my eyes, and a teacher passing by couldn't do a thing with me – I sobbed.

That night I went to bed thinking terrible thoughts as to what should happen to the thief. Saturday morning came, the sun shining through the bedroom curtains, beckoning me to get out of bed. I couldn't face my toast and marmalade: I dressed, washed my face and set off to sulk on my own somewhere away from people. At this moment in time, I hated everyone and everything, but with no one to really blame.

I was kicking a tin along the path through the allotments, taking it out on the tin I suppose, the end of my right shoe turning white as I rubbed off the black polish on the leather.

Quite suddenly a man rushed by on a cycle, pushing me into the privet hedge, the hedge breaking my fall. 'I know that bike!' I said as I got up off the broken privet hedge, 'that's my three-speeder!' But before I could shout, the man was gone. I ran breathless through the streets and into the town to find a policeman, my heart beating a crescendo in my rib cage.

'I've seen it, I've seen it!' I shouted at the policeman, fighting back the tears. 'Now then me lad!' said the policeman, 'calm down and take your time, what's this all about?'

'I've seen my bike!' I yelled in his face, 'there's a man on my bike. My Raleigh three-speeder is down Ripley fields, a man's riding it.' 'Right, let's get to a phone and get a patrol car on the job,' he said, grabbing my hand and stepping off at a fast pace. Within a matter of minutes, a car arrived, a Wolsley, all black and shiny.

The door opened, and out stepped a constable, towering over me like the genie from Aladdin's lamp. 'Come along my lad, get in – let's see if we can find this bike o'yawn,' he said in broad Derbyshire accent. 'Hasster ever seen this bloke before? He'll most likely a gone bi nar.'

'Crikey,' I thought, as we made our way around the busy town, 'what will the people think as I sit here between two policemen? Will they think I've been arrested?' We toured the town, but to no avail: both man and bike had disappeared, as if off the face of the earth. Tears started to flow as I sat in the car, both the driver and the sergeant next to me trying to comfort me.

Anyway, I thought, not many kids at school get a ride in a police car.! The police dropped me off at home, with half the street turning out to see what Staley's lad had been up to. Sunday passed by, and I didn't even bother to go out to play with my friends.

On arrival at school on the Monday morning, all the different classes had to form up in the playground: something was up! I could see the headmaster surrounded by teachers, and a familiar face, that of the constable I had run crying to in the town. There was a deathly hush, and then the headmaster shouted, 'Staley!'

'Sir,' I replied, and made my way to the front of the whole school. The policeman held a bike, and I was asked if I recognised it. 'Yes sir! It's mine,' I said, 'I would know it anywhere.' The policeman handed over the cycle to me, and then to my amazement the headmaster gave the whole school a lecture on observation and what action to take, stating how clever I had been in giving a description of the thief, and the Raleigh Sturmey Archer three-speed bike.

The appearance of the bike had been altered, but I would have known that bike anywhere, especially after the love and care I had put into keeping it clean. The constable thanked me for all the information I had given them, and said I would be called upon to attend court.

On arriving home that day, my dad said how lucky I had been to get my bike, but why the glum face? 'Well dad, it's not the same bike really is it? I mean, that chap's messed it about hasn't he?' That bike was never the same for me, I felt as though it had been contaminated. The love for my three-speeder was gone, and once again I was in the doldrums, as my mother called them.

A week or so later, I was told of a job at a local chip shop, and I raced round before anyone else could beat me to it. The lady knew me, and my family, that went a long way towards getting the job in those days. The shop was the terminus for the Midland General, one of the leading bus companies in the district, and that meant the shop was always pretty busy.

My job consisted of chopping the chips on a hand machine, and assisting with the eyeing of the potatoes after they had been in the peeler. The wage was £12 6s, long before decimalisation, and I was determined to save for a brand-new bike. Week after week I saved until I had the princely sum of £5, all in brand new notes. The hours were long, but I enjoyed the work, especially as the lady of the shop had two daughters about my age, one of whom I lost my heart to: my first romance, not very exciting in a chip shop – and it was touch and go which came first, the bike or the dark-haired girl with the beautiful dark eyes.

Both daughters had to help in the shop, as did their brother who was that bit older than me. Their father had died some years before, leaving the mother to fend for her children as best she knew how. It was wartime, and we had the American troops with us, but that is another story! I do remember that well-known saying, 'have you got any gum chum?' Sweets were very scarce, rationed in fact.

To get back to the bike, I happened to be going up Ripley one day, and as I passed this shop window, a cycle caught my eye. A red bike! Red and chrome, with a fixed gear on the rear wheel. It was marvellous, drop handle bars, a pump, a bell, and racing clips on the pedals to strap your feet in. The bike was a Daytona racing cycle, made in Great Britain of course; we made the best bikes in the world. The temptation was too great; I made my way to the shop door and went in. There was a tinkle as I entered the doorway; a bell over the door rang to let the shopkeeper know when someone wanted serving.

'Hello young man! What can I do for you?' the man said when I entered the room. 'Can I have a closer look at the red bike please?' I said. 'Certainly, young man; are you thinking of buying it?' he said with a smile. I think he was only trying to humour me. I spent a long two minutes examining the red racing bike and I knew it was MINE.

Coal and Hot Engine Oil

The very first time I clapped eyes on Monty Buxton was at Ripley Colliery, a No. 4 shovel in his hands and a mouth as big as Portsmouth, later to become my dear friend and workmate. How we came to be such close friends I'll never know, as I was the one in competition with him for being able to talk more. It was said I could talk the hind legs off a donkey.

Being on the coalface, a stint of coal (twenty-six tonnes) was blood, sweat and tears, but we were the richest lads in the town. Our deputy, a man named Sid Gibson, looked on us as his boys. While at work there wasn't anything we wouldn't do for him. His means of transport being a 500cc single AJS which I almost ruined for him, but that's another story – a black day for me.

Monty's grandmother kept the Gate Inn at Lower Hartshay, a lovely old lady who stood no nonsense from the customers. In the back of the pub were some sheds, fowl sheds by the look of them, and being asked to go and visit, I was dying to know what was in one of the sheds. My friend Monty pushed open a battered shed door, which was leaning on one rusty hinge; as we entered the shed, there on its prop stand was a black enamelled 'Gold Flash', a 650cc bike, the pride of BSA. I was spellbound as I sat side-saddle on that magnificent machine. Cyril (Cibble)

Opposite above: No. 4, Derek Minter, No. 50, Monty Buxton, No. 44, Phil Reed.

Opposite below: My daughter Jayne on a borrowed bike.

Right: Side-car racing at Mallory Park in the 1950s.

Below: Donington.

Cadwell Park, Lincolnshire.

My father, Leslie Staley, on
my 500cc dominator.

Chamberlain had a 500cc apple-green 'Shooting Star', and he and Monty rode together. We must have walked around this bike at least half a dozen times taking in all the latest fittings. When we were out on the road everyone stopped to admire these beautiful machines; later I bought a 650cc Gold Flash with the original gold colour – I couldn't resist it.

It wasn't long before Monty was experimenting with high-compression pistons and altering gear ratios. Speed was what all three of us wanted, especially me, and as much noise as the police would allow with their decibel counters. As a result, the courts were a regular haunt for Staley's lad: I was on speaking terms with most of the constables. I well remember my mother wringing her hands at the gate and shouting to people in the street to stand clear. She could hear me half a mile away as I made my way home from Denby Hall pit baths; because we had no baths at Ripley pit, we had to move to Denby Hall. The area is now a factory and, just below that, a new hotel.

Further down on the other side is Denby Pottery, and weren't we pleased when the pits closed owing to the seams of coal running out. Monty and I worked in the piper and black shale seams. When it closed, some men were set on at Denby Pottery. I went to Moorgreen, Eastwood, a member of the hated 'Spencer Union'.

Monty took the plunge and went freelance, a market trader in nylons and knitwear. It was rough for a time, and Monty, his wife Sheila, and my wife and I worked all hours to make a go of it. He bought a Volkswagon van, a 1600cc light blue model from Derby, and we were off. I was part-time of course, casual until we got a regular stall. Once I slept in the van all night in 2ft of snow to be first casual on the Saturday morning, the market being the coldest place on earth.

Before he started trading, Monty got hold of a BSA Gold Star, a racer if ever there was one!! Come Friday after work, off would come the lights, the headlamp, the kick-start pedal, the lot: anything to lighten the bike.

We were going racing. Alton Towers was our objective: that sleepy little place didn't know what hit it! The revs on the bike were sent racing up and down, the rev counter trying to burst its way out of the casing. This was the beginning of a long friendship with Harry Middleton of Ripley, a brilliant engineer who worked for Rolls Royce during the war. After BSAs Monty went on to Manx Nortons, helped and owned by Mr Whippy, the ice-cream man.

While racing at Mallory Park, Monty had an accident: the front brake callipers that operate the shoes failed. He came off at what is known as the ESSS and whilst on the track Joe Dumphy rode over his leg and broke it.

During this period of time (1963) while we were at race meetings, we met all the greats: Bob McIntye, Derek Minter, Alan Shepherd and many more, including Geoff Duke, John Surtees and Giacimo Agustieney. Bill Lomas was the only one who could handle the eight-cylinder Motto Guzzi. When Bill left the starting line no one could live with him. The Japanese had merely got started with Mike Hailwood and his record-breaking 250cc Honda.

Many, many times I stood in the pit yard at Denby Hall selling oil at 12s 6d a gallon, Castrol XL, Castrol XXL and the Castor 'R' which Monty kept for his 350 and 500 Nortons. Monty still has these bikes today, and every now and again they come out of mothballs and are raced at Cadwell near Louth, Notts.

It's Not My Fault

Having the gift of the gab, I decided as a union man that I was a likely candidate for the town council. The thought crossed my mind I couldn't be any worse than the shower who'd already been elected, so I went and got chosen for the Ripley and Waingroves Ward.

Duly elected, I was amazed how popular one became as a councillor. Depending on what shift I was on, I was told in no uncertain terms to attend half an hour before the press arrived as there were things to talk over. Being my first meeting I decided all on my own to remain quiet and take on board what was being discussed. All went well until our leader said, 'right, that's it then, you all stick your hands up and follow me!' Not being one to rock the boat, I was eased into the chamber and shown my seat.

The meeting carried on through the agenda until someone mentioned spending money on the leisure centre. I saw red and the next moment I was on my feet, arms up in the air and flailing about. 'Mr Chairman! Mr Chairman!' I shouted, 'the damn thing shouldn't even have been built in the first place, not there anyway!' Originally it was built and partly paid for by the townspeople but then it was taken over by the district council. Even before a brick was laid I advised them it would be a disaster to build on the plot pegged out.

Once again I spoke to deaf ears – in fact, I was told to sit down. You'll never guess, on a show of hands the work was to commence. I once again went into a huddle with the press and repeated what I had said many times: the ground was unstable owing to the close proximity of Ripley pit.

How do I know this? Well, being a coalface worker on the black shale and piper seams of coal, one day I had cleaned out the slack where the cutter had gone through on the night shift, applying nogs of wood to stand the weight of the coal above the cut. When this was done, I shouted down the face for the shot-firer, an official who places pellets of explosive into the holes made in the coal by the chap with the electric borer.

We retreated down the face, one man going in the opposite direction. One almighty shout of 'fire' and there was an ear-shattering explosion followed by a bank of thick, choking dust, the ventilation system taking ages to clear; the dust blowing out towards the upcast shaft, the downcast bringing in the life-giving fresh air from a huge fan set in a tunnel into the shaft side.

The face conveyor was still racing along the face and as I got on, sneaking a ride which broke all the safety rules, I found myself in something which I can only describe as a huge cave. This was the disaster I dreaded – this huge hole, this cave of coal had turned into a 30ft face of gleaming, mirror-shining coal you could see to shave in. I was looking at the end of the Pennine chain, a fault in the earth causing a slip of 25-30ft between the seams of coal.

My deputy Sid Gibson came about twenty minutes later, followed by a phone call to our senior 'over man', Wilf Sparham, a lovely man who stood no nonsense from anyone. This was his pit. Wilf has just passed away at the age of ninety-two years. He came to Ripley from Brittain pit upon its closure, this pit holding the world record for tonnage of coal turned up in a 9ft shaft, never to be beaten.

In the 1990s, or possibly before, cracks appeared in the brick columns either side of the main doorway of the leisure centre. The brickwork was inspected after I reported it to the local paper, *The Ripley and Heanor News*, and metal strips were inserted into the cracks to check on movement.

Anyway, the top and bottom of it is, after all my warnings, the leisure centre is to be demolished – but a new one is being built not a stone's throw away, at the back of the old site. This reminds me of the nursery rhyme: 'all the king's horses and all the king's men'… I rest my case.

Romance on a 650CC Motorcycle

This story begins at South Normanton Welfare. I was with a young lady and ready to try out my new dance steps. Being on the coalface, money was the least of my worries. I had been to Derby

Keith Staley meets Keith Staley

● **Keith Leslie Staley (left) meets Keith Vincent Staley (right) for the very first time, at the home of Keith Leslie in Heage. MD28886.**

KEITH Staley of Horsley Woodhouse meets his namesake living in Heage - for the very first time!

News readers will be familiar with Keith Leslie Staley of High Edge Drive, Heage - once a Ripley Town

Councillor - who still writes regularly to the paper.

The Keith Staley of Horsley Woodhouse - Keith Vincent - began to think about his distant relations last year, when his daughter Helen asked him to start investigating their family tree.

He said: "When the name of Arthur Staley came into view I remembered a photo I had seen in a book some years before, with an Arthur and his wife on a motorbike.

"I asked everyone I knew about books of the area and one day a friend produced a book - Ripley and Codnor - by David Buxton.

"There on page 85 was the photo.

"I then found photos in the book of more Staleys including Keith Staley, whose name is included amongst the acknowledgements, and concluded that he and I were indeed related."

On February 13 Keith Vincent wrote to Keith Leslie of Heage and asked if he would be interested in getting together

● **Keith Vincent Staley (left) pores over old family pictures with Keith Leslie Staley. MD28885**

to talk about their ancestors for mutual enjoyment, and see if any gaps could be filled regarding their activities and relationships.

The two Keiths finally met for the very first time last week at High Edge Drive. They discovered they were related through their grandfathers. Keith Vincent's grandfather - Alfred Robert - was the younger brother to Arthur Staley - grandfather to Keith Leslie.

Keith Vincent Staley, who had no idea that the Ripley and Heanor News pho-

tographer would snap the occasion said: "It was a surprise that our meeting would be recorded like this.

"We had a wonderful time, and spent 2½ hours together.

"We got on really well, and we will definitely be meeting up again.

Keith Leslie said: "All my friends wanted to see a picture of my namesake, and this was the perfect opportunity."

The two Keiths are now on the trail of the origin of the family - were they from Ripley, or London?

New service launched

A NEW Mencap Pathway Employment Service for Derbyshire and Derby City has been launched.

The event was held at the Rolls - Royce Sport and Leisure Centre.

It featured a talk by Steve Park-

er of the Heanor Gate Association.

The Mencap Pathway service offers help and support to people with learning disabilities to access training, education, voluntary work, work experience and paid employment.

Causing headlines! The story above, published on the 4 March 2004, reveals how our grandfathers were brothers; below is the header of one of my letters highlighting the local need for a memorial for miners.

Ripley mining memorial need

Above: Keith and Rose Staley.

Below: Me on a Gold Flash, £357 new.

the day before and bought a new suit – and not just any old suit, but what the Americans call a tuxedo. There I was in all my glory, black patent shoes, a satin stripe down the legs of the trousers, immaculate white shirt and a black bow tie. The young lady hung on to my arm as though we were glued together: her name was Mary. Mary's father was the local bookmaker, and many's the time he would come home late at night: it wasn't difficult to weigh up whether or not he had had a good day at the races. He wore a check coat and corduroy trousers that had seen many a muddy track. No sooner had he sat down he would say, 'In't it time you were going, lad?'

To get back to the welfare and dance, the band would strike up: the first was usually a quickstep and I would be on my feet like a shot. Mary clung to me as we passed a group of her school friends. The girls were giggling and tittering, as I was something special in my new suit. To be honest I looked as though I was one of the band. The dance hadn't been announced as an 'excuse me', but that didn't stop one of the girls touching Mary's arm and stopped us dancing for a moment. 'Excuse me,' said this beautiful girl, ignoring Mary and gazing straight into my eyes, 'do you mind?' Our eyes met, and I could see my reflection in her eyes and in that instant I knew this was the girl of my dreams. We danced as close as two peas in a pod. My dancing teacher believed there should only be the thickness of a bus ticket between two people dancing, and who was I to argue?

The dance ended and Mary and I made our way to the door, my new 650cc Gold Flash motorcycle gleaming in the light from the open door. Mary lived about 100 yards from the dance hall, and a row of cottages lined her street, built, I should imagine, for the miners who worked at the collieries in the area. I straddled the bike, pushed off the prop stand and Mary got on the pillion seat. Two minutes later I dropped her off outside the cottage, said cheerio and kicked up the bike. Waiting till she was safely inside I turned the bike round and returned to where the girls were chatting, putting on their coats. Nowhere could I find the girl who had cheekily excused herself and cut in. I asked all the girls, but to no avail: she had gone, and I revved the bike in frustration. 'You can give me a lift,' said one of the girls, and with that got on the pillion. Five minutes later I was back... but the excitement of a bike ride had attracted them and they formed a queue! I was informed the young girl I had taken a shine to was a shy sixteen year old named Rose.

I didn't see her again for about three years, but my brother-in-law's sister told me she had been knocked down by a car at the age of seventeen. Rose had stepped off a bus and walked behind it and was knocked down. Joyce and Rose worked together in a dress shop owned by a lady named Eva Thorpe. Apparently later Rose became very ill, losing a lot of weight and eventually having to be admitted into Mansfield General Hospital at nineteen. She had to have a serious operation; she was then the youngest person to have this operation at the general (in 1956).

Apparently Rose was in hospital for many months. She was then transferred to Debdale Recovery Hospital at Mansfield Woodhouse, where she stayed for another five months: she was in bed for most of the time because she was very weak.

Sometime after she came home from Debdale I met her again when she came with a friend to a dance at the Drill Hall, Alfreton. The band was Victor Sylvestor's. I couldn't resist dancing to the world's greatest strict dance tempo. I took Rose home from the dance and we began seeing each other.

Rose later had to go back into hospital with a skin complaint resulting from the operation. I visited frequently, taking cream roses which cheered her up tremendously. We married at St Michael's church South Normanton in December 1957 and will celebrate our golden wedding this year (2007) with our daughter, son-in-law, son, daughter-in-law, three grandchildren and friends. The years have been good to us; Rose worked for twenty-one years at a residential home for the elderly at Alfreton. Looking after the elderly seems some sort of repayment for all the time spent in hospital. Thank God for a National Health Service that was there for my wife.

Gertie and Les in Skegness, 1939.

South Normanton Miners' Welfare.

One brick remains: all that is left of South Normanton Miners' Welfare.

Left: Mr Wilfred Sparham, who gave me my first job on the coalface. Senior overman.

Below: 350cc Matchless, Rose Staley with Jayne and my bike. One of many!

This page: The wedding of Raymond Fletcher, MP.

Above: 'Middle pub', Waingroves. Mother with 'Lizzie' Cope and Jayne Staley.

Opposite above: Tram Museum, Crich: in the photo are Rose and my grandaughter, Samantha.

Opposite below: Crich.

My Norton 500cc twin.

Butterley Swanwick junction.

Ripley Railway Museum.

An old Midland General bus in the car park.

Rose, Keith and Rachel.

Above: Western fan, Butterley.

Opposite: Miners' holiday camp in Rhyl, 1940. Dad and a friend.

Above: South Normanton church, where I married on 26 December 1957.

Opposite: London for the cup final in 1946. Me with mother and Aunt Edith.

Ormonde Colliery. Ross Parkin and Fred Osbourne are in the middle; at the front are dad and Les Staley.

Above: The old water tower, South Normanton.

Right: Pit Lane junction, Waingroves.

Pumping Station, Ernest Hall.

Here I am with my cousin, Peter Sharp.

Above: Ford's pumping pit, Marehay.

Opposite: Headstocks at Ford's pit, made at the Butterley Works in 1947.

Sago in a Teapot: Ford's Pit Pumping Station

It was 1946 and I had just completed my training at Hartshay Training Centre off Heage Road, Ripley. Percy Alton was in charge of training. I had been at school with his son Tom, my friend who became an electrician just before nationalisation. We passed out with flying colours; Mr Alton kept a special eye on us.

On completion of the course, I joined 'Billy Eyre's' gang of odd sods and bods. Fitters and electricians, rope splicers, welders, blacksmiths – you name it, they could handle it.

We had our own means of transport, an American Ford V8 car with the rear of the car chopped off and made into a van. Ross Parkin was the driver-cum-fitter-cum-climber-cum anything else asked of him: a glint every day in his eyes, a smile for everyone but his brother Harry, who was that bit older and second in command. I never did find out why two brothers couldn't get on, wishing my brother had lived at birth.

The year was 1946 and I remember when we arrived at Ford's pit. We entered a field by some large wooden gates opposite Marehay Cricket Ground, and nearby was a huge American army lorry, a dodge, I think. The lorry was being used to carry coal, but still was painted a dull grey-brown, with a white star on the doors.

We passed through the first field and then had to stop as a car emerged from a row of cottages to the right of us in the second field. With a surge of power from the V8 engine, throwing five men into a tangled heap and swearing as only colliers do, I looked out onto the ruts we had left in the snow, the snow we dreaded: the field we were heading for had freezing grass and nothing else. It was going to be our job to build a pumping station from scratch.

At about 10.30 a.m., a Butterley low-loader lorry arrived with a heap of angle irons and sheets of asbestos. British workmen never start work till they've had a brew. My job was to go to the cottages for water while they got a fire going. It wasn't long before we were warmed up with a mug of strong tea with plenty of sugar and we were ready to start erecting a fitting shop.

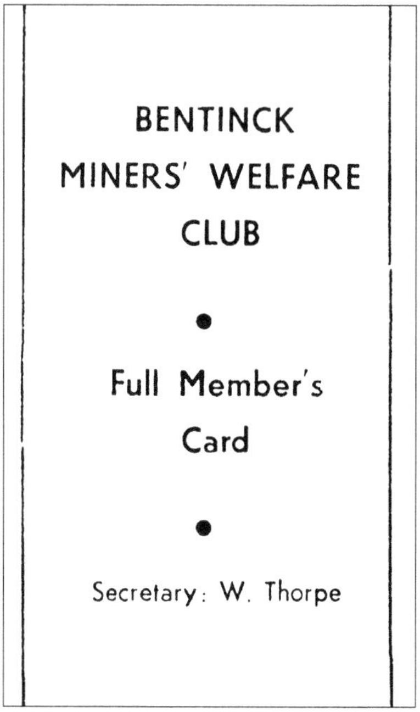

BENTINCK
MINERS' WELFARE
CLUB

•

Full Member's
Card

•

Secretary: W. Thorpe

Bentinck Miners' Welfare Club membership, including my 'motty' number, Brentwick Colly.

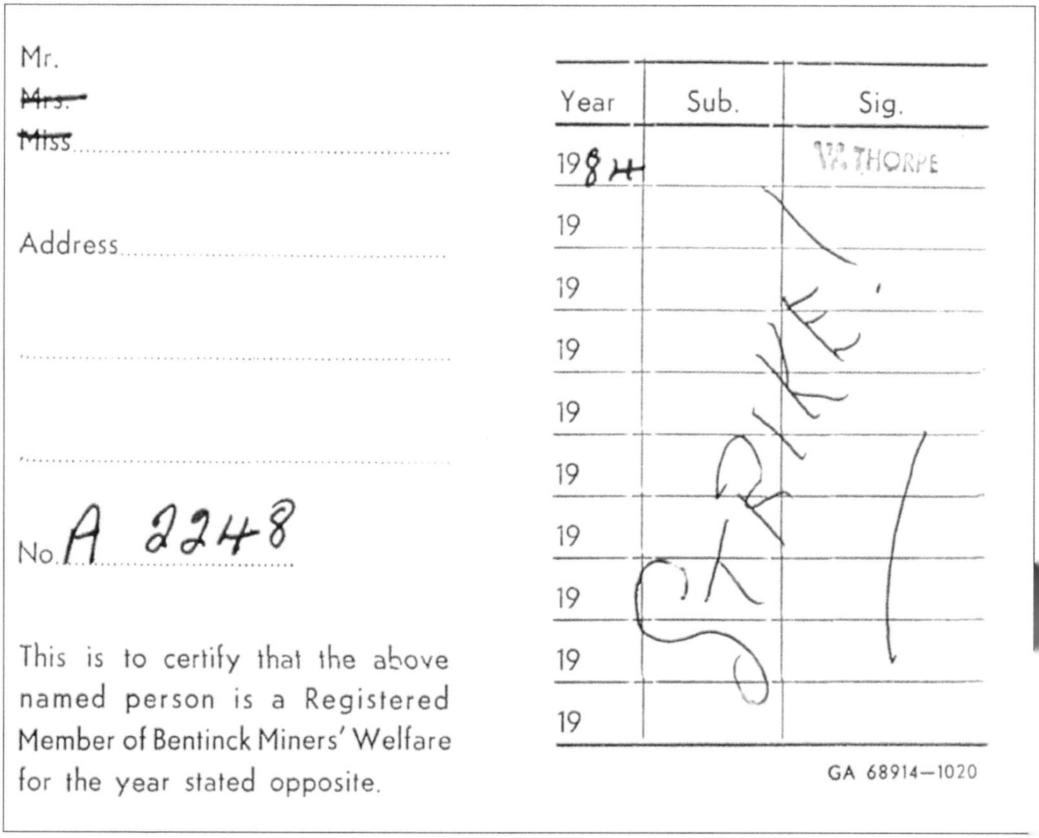

Mr.
~~Mrs.~~
~~Miss~~...

Address................................

....

....

No. A 2248

This is to certify that the above named person is a Registered Member of Bentinck Miners' Welfare for the year stated opposite.

Year	Sub.	Sig.
198H		W. THORPE
19		
19		
19		
19		
19		
19		
19		
19		
19		

GA 68914—1020

As time passed and we were getting some spring weather, a lorry arrived with an upright boiler. Old Ernie Hall soon got cracking and in no time at all we had the steam up. The engine house was near completion and the headstocks had arrived via Ripley town centre. A large derrick pole was put in place and we erected two 80ft steel legs. Next up were the tying-in girders, which had to be bolted together ready for the next two legs still on the ground to be attached. To climb the girders, you insert your knees in the groove of the girders, and your toes on the outside, applying pressure as you climb.

To bolt the two legs together, any sane person would have come down one leg and up the other. Now bear in mind it was frosty and had been snowing earlier: Ross, without any thought of danger, JUMPED from one leg to the other! 80ft of fresh air, what a stupid but breathtaking thing to do: talk about a monkey, his snap must have consisted of bananas. On coming down, Mr Eyre gave him the biggest telling off (he couldn't sack him as he was our means of getting to and from home).

Summer arrived and the headstocks were complete: now all we were waiting for was the huge steel rope to lower and raise the SULTCER pumps. The pumps had been reclaimed from Bushes Scrap Yard at Birchwood Lane, Somercotes. The pump and huge electric motor had to be fitted into a cradle to be lifted and lowered as rainfall filled the shaft from many different sources and cascaded down the old worn brickwork of the shaft.

It was a twenty-four hour ordeal as pipes had to be put on and taken off at the drop of a hat. Now, at Salterwood, German 'Harland Wolf' pumps and motors remained on the surface, and only pipes remained in the shaft, with a steel driving shaft (held by metal spiders) going to the ochre, red and yellow water from the old workings.

Bernard Parr and his sister lived in a bungalow at the shaft-side. I'm talking 1946. German prisoners of war cleared Salterwood to make a spoil heap for Denby Hall, Washery (now a brand-new hotel) on a site almost facing Denby Pottery. To get back to Ford's, our electrician was Mr Godkin; he sold all the prams and toys in Ripley from a shop at the corner of Church Street. Harry was his name, a lovely, well-mannered gentleman. I sit here thinking of the time I almost poisoned the lot of them.

I made the tea with water I got from a stream. Dare I say it, the kettle boiled up full of frogspawn: to this day I still sweat at the thought of what I did to my workmates. Staley's lad was in dead trouble! I had to hope and pray word didn't get to our chief, Mr Edgar Drabble.

Long before anyone had an automatic gearbox in their car, Mr Drabble was experimenting with the idea. The poor man, he tried to teach me algebra but it wouldn't sink in, I was a pick-and-shovel man. I must have been a great loss to Butterley Company.

Above: Ford's pit, 1946. (I am holding the spanner).

Opposite and below: London, and the cup final of the same year.

REME & RAVC RECORD OFFICE,
Glen Parva Barracks,
South Wigston,
LEICESTER.
Tel: WIGSTON 89621 Ext 31
DIV II/HEO/Recall/S.R.
30| 9 | 1952   ('7)

2/88

To:- 22405041 Pte K1. Staley
29 Wrights Ave.
Ripley Derbys.

Subject: Supplementary Reserve
Instruction Book AB 334

    The attached Army Book 334 "Supplementary Reservist's Instruction" is forwarded to you for retention so long as you are serving in the Supplementary Reserve.

    Your attention is requested to the front cover of AB 334 in regard to the necessity for keeping this document clean and in a safe place when not in use.

    Immediately you receive the book turn to Page 6 and insert your National Insurance Number in the place provided in Part 'A'. Part 'B' will not be completed until you rejoin the Colours.

    Page 9 and 10 are only completed when you rejoin, and also Pages 11 and 13 are for your use on Mobilization only.

    This Book is of the utmost importance to you, and must be safeguarded. In the event of your being recalled to the Colours, you are required to hand it in to your Unit. Should you never be recalled to the Colours the book must be returned to the OIC Records on completion of your period of service in the Supplementary Reserve.

    If this book is lost or stolen, the facts will be reported immediately to this office.

    It is also emphasised that any change of your private address should be notified to this office immediately. (See Para 2 of "Instructions" inside front cover).

E.O.
COL,
REME & RAVC RECORDS.

1950 National Service; 1952 REME.

NOTICE TO BE GIVEN TO A MAN COMPLETING SERVICE IN THE REGULAR, RESERVE, OR AUXILIARY FORCES WHO WILL BECOME A MAN OF THE ARMY RESERVE UNDER SECTION I OF THE NAVY, ARMY AND AIR FORCE RESERVES ACT, 1954.

To :

No. *2240507*. Rank *Pte.* Surname *Staley*

Christian or Fore Name(s) *Keith Leslie* Regt./Corps *R.E.M.E*

You are hereby notified that on completing your engagement of *National Service* in the *Army* you will become a member of the Army Reserve, Class I (Army General Reserve (Group *N*)) by virtue of the provisions of the Navy, Army and Air Force Reserves Act, 1954, and that, unless previously discharged from that Reserve, you will remain a member of that Reserve until 30th June, 1959 or until you attain the age of forty-five years, whichever is the earlier.

You are hereby warned that as a man of the Army General Reserve you will be subject to the following liabilities :—

(1) To be called out on permanent service by proclamation of Her Majesty in Council under Section 5 of the Army Reserve Act, 1950, in case of imminent national danger or great emergency ; when so called out you will be liable *to serve in the United Kingdom or elsewhere.*

(2) To be called out on permanent service by the direction of a Secretary of State under Section 6 (1) (*a*) of the Army Reserve Act, 1950, for service at any place *in the United Kingdom* in defence of the United Kingdom against actual or apprehended attack.

*(3) To notify to the authority stated within fourteen days of being required to do so by notice in writing sent to you by or on behalf of the Army Council, your name and address and certain particulars relating to your occupation or qualifications which will be specified in the notice.

You will not be liable to be called out in aid of the civil power under Section 10 of the Army Reserve Act, 1950, nor for any form of training.

You will not be entitled to receive any pay during your service in the Army General Reserve unless you are called out on permanent service.

*You are requested to inform the Officer in charge of your Record Office of any change in your permanent address.

Official Stamp

HANTS.

(50102) WT.37390/4915 380,000 2/54 A.& E.W.LTD. GP.677

1950/1952, Honiton, Devon.

(Only to be completed in cases of service with the
Colours, i.e., mobilised or embodied service.)

THE FOLLOWING TESTIMONIAL IS BASED ON
THE SOLDIER'S CONDUCT DURING SERVICE
WITH THE COLOURS.

Serial No. 7317

Army Form B.108D

Certificate of Service

Signature and Rank.. Colonel,

Commandant,

H.Q., Officer-i/Army Emergency Reserve, R.E.M.E. Records

Date E 6 MAR 1956 Place...................... LONDON

(48017) WT.36859/3974 80,000 3/53 A.& E.W.LTD. GP.698

WARNING

Soldiers on quitting Her Majesty's Service are hereby
reminded that the unauthorised communication by them
to another person AT ANY TIME of any information they
may have acquired which might be useful to an enemy in
War renders them liable to prosecution under the Official
Secrets Acts.

The person to whom this Certificate is issued should on no
account part with it or forward it by post when applying
for a situation but should use a copy attested by a
responsible person for the purpose. If the Certificate is
lost it will be replaced only when its loss can be proved
to have been due to very exceptional circumstances.
Application for replacement should be made to the Officer-
in-charge, Records, concerned.

Any alteration of the particulars given on this Certificate
may render the holder liable to prosecution under the
Seamen's and Soldiers' False Character Act, 1906.

ANY PERSON finding this Certificate is requested
to forward it in an unstamped envelope to :—

THE UNDER-SECRETARY OF STATE,
THE WAR OFFICE,
LONDON,
S.W.1.

Above and below: The papers for 22405071, PTE Staley.

These pages should be entirely free from erasure

THIS IS TO CERTIFY THAT :—

Christian or
Fore Name(s) Keith Leslie.

Surname Staley.

Army No. 22405071. Rank Pte.

Army Emergency Reserve

was discharged from* 6 3 56.

Para 108(xviii)B AE Regs 1956 in consequence of
TERMINATION OF ENGAGEMENT

Corps from which discharged R.E.M.E.

He also served during this engagement in (Corps)

Date of birth 20/5/32

Signature
of Soldier

Medals, Clasps, Decorations, Mentions in Despatches.
Any special acts of gallantry or distinguished conduct
brought to notice in Brigade or superior orders :—

THE PARTICULARS WHICH FOLLOW
REFER ONLY TO THE ENGAGEMENT
FROM WHICH HE/SHE IS NOW
BEING DISCHARGED

Deemed { at for Part Time Service in A.E.R.
Enlisted { on 22/ 9/ 19 52.

He/She has served :—
(a) With the Colours Nil years
Nil days

(b) In* ARMY EMERGENCY RESERVE
Three years One hundred
and forty six days

* Here insert " Army Emergency Reserve," or " Territorial
Army," as the case may be.

[P.T.O.

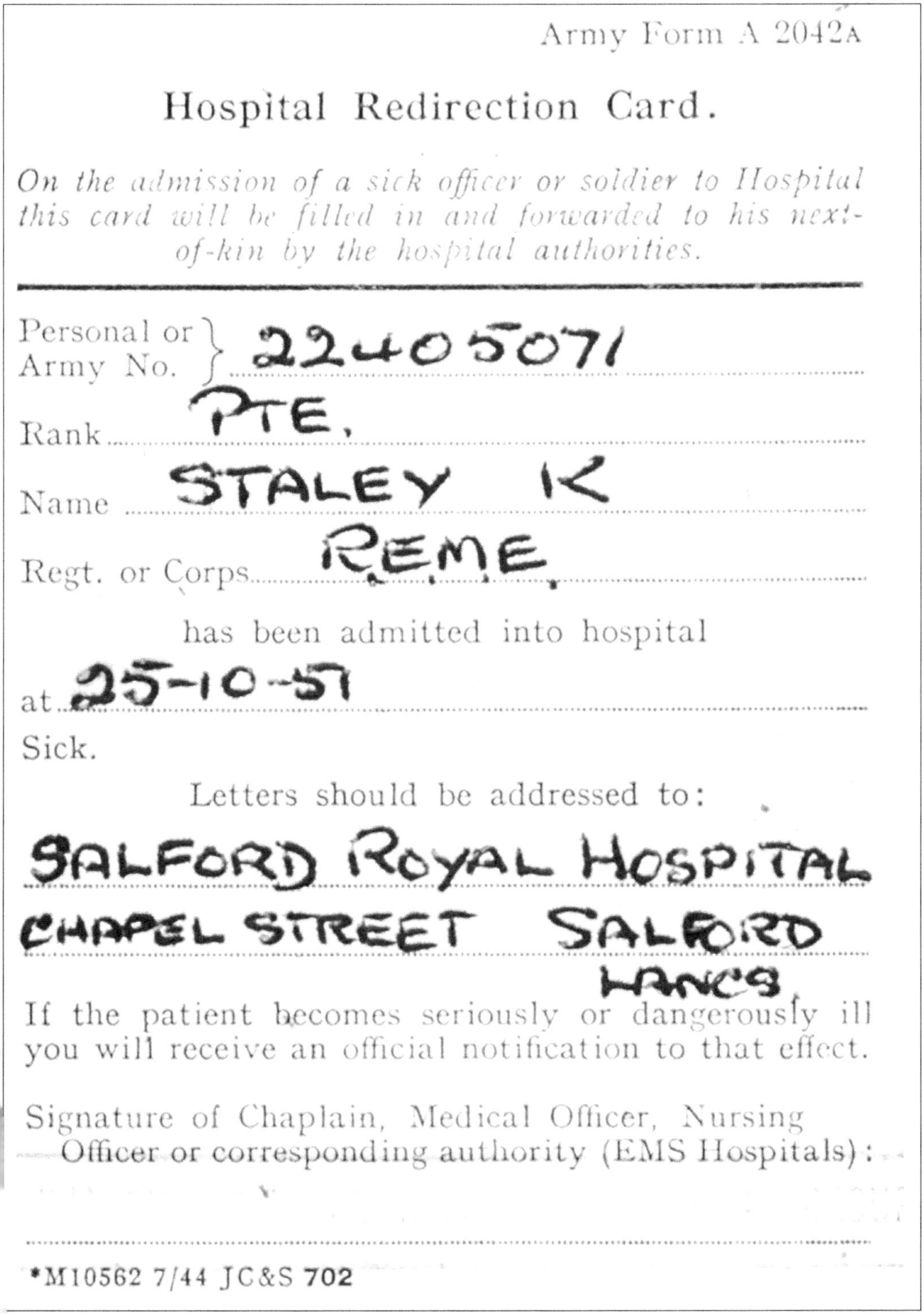

Army Form A 2042A

Hospital Redirection Card.

On the admission of a sick officer or soldier to Hospital this card will be filled in and forwarded to his next-of-kin by the hospital authorities.

Personal or Army No. } 22405071

Rank PTE.

Name STALEY K

Regt. or Corps REME

has been admitted into hospital

at 25-10-57

Sick.

Letters should be addressed to:

SALFORD ROYAL HOSPITAL
CHAPEL STREET SALFORD
LANCS.

If the patient becomes seriously or dangerously ill you will receive an official notification to that effect.

Signature of Chaplain, Medical Officer, Nursing Officer or corresponding authority (EMS Hospitals):

*M10562 7/44 JC&S 702

Hospital under Mr Poole Wilson, surgeon. Passed 'A1' for the Army.

Above: Butterley Railway Museum.

Opposite above: The cup final again: mum and dad, Aunty Eva, Aunty Lizzie.

Opposite below: Dad's convalescent home in Skegness (he is circled).

ON HIS MAJESTY'S SERVICE.

The Officer i/c _____ Records,

             R.E.M.E. & R.A.V.C. RECORDS,

at _____ GLEN PARVA BARRACKS.

             WIGSTON, LEICESTER.

THE WAR OFFICE.

Above: 'On His Majesty's Service'. War office document from 1950–1952.

Below: The other Keith Staley – 'Vincent', whose story is on page 29, is on the far right.

The Hippodrome, the old cinema in High Street, Ripley. 1s 9d for the back row...

Yesterday's Dreams

The days and nights passed very slowly as I tried very hard, searching the shops for a DVD... and not just any old DVD, but a copy of the 1938 classic, *Robin Hood*. Many, many times as a little boy I watched Errol Flynn and Olivia de Havilland running through Sherwood Forest to escape Basil Rathbone, playing Guy Gisbourne, the evil Sheriff of Nottingham.

As a boy I used to fence with the boy next door. My sword was made from a Lurpak butter barrel, and my bow and arrows were taken from the garden privet hedge. My hands cut and bleeding with splinters, mother would fetch me into a warm kitchen fed by a collier's fire, and wash and bathe my wounds before sending me off to bed, ready to renew my battle with the sheriff the next day!

Little John, real name John Little, I remember, had to fight Robin before he was accepted into the band of outlaws. A quarter staff was his sturdy weapon. Mine?! A brush handle minus the brush.

Age is no limit to the mind: seventy-four years old now, balding on top, dentures, and every other word 'pardon', my hearing gone, fizzled out with the coal dust and mining machinery, but nevertheless my heart still pounds as I watch Robin climb up a gnarled old vine to Maid Marion's window. The embrace and the kiss captured everything of Shakespeare's *Romeo and Juliet*.

I used to put my father, bless him, into the role of Robin Hood, but instead of a bow and a sword, dad would be wielding his sturdy riveting hammer. Being a boilersmith with his hammer, the Sheriff of Nottingham would not have stood a chance.

Butterley Co. was our main source of income and to some extent acted as King Richard's brother, John, offering wages instead of taxes. Their castle was Butterley Hall, now Derbyshire Police Headquarters. We were far from posh, although mother had a brand-new Treadle Singer sewing machine, and dad a Raleigh three-speeder bike.

Keith and Rose.

To get back to dad, long before compressed-air hammers, as used in the shipyards, my grandad, my dad and his stepbrother would renew the Lancashire boilers and prepare them for the inspector. As a boy and later a man, I must admit that Errol Flynn, although my favourite, couldn't hold a candle to my dad.

Whilst I was attending the local Empire cinema, dad worked all the hours that God sent so we could enjoy a week at Skegness Miner's Holiday Camp. So much per week would be stopped from his wages, money for transport and accommodation.

The sea was great, the sand was smashing, but if *Robin Hood* was showing, who cared? Mother knew where to find me, quite safe, wishing I was in Sherwood Forest. Now in my later years, with an active mind, but a body gone to pot, I sit and dream of what might have been, a pit boy taken off to America, to MGM Universal Studios, to act among the stars of the 1930s and 1940s.

Fascination

Please, let me introduce you to my boyhood world of fascination, my world of gangsters. As a boy of eight or nine my dad took my to see all the great stars of that period: to name just a few, my favourite would be Edward G. Robinson, a great actor that could put the fear of God into you just by the sound of his voice. That small fat man with a scowl always on his face, a large Cuban cigar wedged in the corner of his mouth, 'oh the joy of seeing a re-run', first and second house if dad wasn't on early shift. Humphrey Bogart was absolutely smashing, especially in the same film as Claire Trevor and Lauren Bacall. *Key Largo* was great: the youngsters of today think they have it all with their Japanese gimmicks but the thrill of these superstars remains for us today thanks to the gadgets we can purchase. Once again, thank you Japan.

Whichever picture house (cinema) I attended, I was guaranteed to come home with a flea. Between the two cinemas, there wasn't much to choose: perhaps the Hippodrome fleas were slightly larger than those of the Empire. On arriving home mother would strip me and put me in a hot bath: this was a novelty as we had moved to a new council house almost in the pit yard. Thereby is another story of horror to be told. When I wasn't in hospital, which wasn't very often, my Saturday was to go to the Saturday matinée. The great thing about the Empire was that my step-grandmother on my dad's side was one of the usherettes.

With a large torch in her hand I had to behave, especially as I had got in for free. Films were almost all cowboys, Johnny McBrown, Roy Rogers and Dale Robertson (not forgetting Trigger, his marvellous horse). I liked Andy Divine, a great big fat man with a squeaky voice. Just pity the poor horse that had to carry Andy and his twenty-three stones!

Talking of pity, what about the children who had to listen to Roy Rogers singing and playing his guitar? I sit today and think of all those Indians who were shot or captured by a man in a huge white Stetson hat, a diamond-studded shirt and cowboy boots with toy guns at either side. He must have spent hours in make up – and no matter how many scrapes he got into his shirt never got torn.

Once the film had finished, the wooden shacks of the town shot to pieces, there would be a mad screaming rush for the exit. Anyone foolish enough to stand near those large brass-handled glass doors would be bowled over. The pavement would be completely covered with young Roy Rogers slapping their thighs as if on a horse. For five minutes there would be sheer bedlam as the children escaped from the sheriff, arms and legs prising their way onto the road.

Today I have it on good authority that Trigger was stuffed after he passed into the great beyond, and is on show in the ranch house of Roy and Dale. Never again are we to see young boys slapping their thighs as they emerge from a flea-ridden picture house. Oh, I remember it well, the fleas, the ice-cream cones we pelted each other with and the toffee wrappers my grandma had to clean up. I want my thoughts of my early days to remain with me forever.

Up, Up And Away

It was early morning, and mist hung about waiting for the sun to break through the low-lying clouds. Raymond was late in arriving; we had arranged to meet up outside the Britannia pub, 'bottom pub' to the locals. I was there with my new bike, a Daytona Speed Master, which I had purchased the day before. (Raymond Webster's father was the bandmaster at Ormonde Colliery).

As I mentioned earlier, my dad couldn't afford a bike for me at the time, so I decided to get a part-time job and buy one myself: the Ripley Midland bus terminus was the place, and Rowbotham's chip shop – twelve and six a week and a bottle of pop for Christmas. The hours were long, 6-11 p.m. on Thursday and Friday nights, 10.30 a.m. to 1.30 p.m. on Saturday morning and 6.30 p.m. to midnight on a Saturday night. We got all the Americans in late as they turned out from the Midland Hotel across the road; a great bunch of lads, especially the black lads, very well-mannered and talkative; only once did we see them out together with their white comrades and then there was hell let loose in our chip shop: how they fought the Nazis together, I'll never know.

Anyway, now to get back to my new bike, no gears, I had a fixed wheel with clips on the pedals to hold my feet in place, two aluminium bottles attached to the handle bars and a bright yellow waterproof strapped to the saddle. Time was of the essence, the mist had lifted and I was getting impatient. When Raymond arrived he was blue in the face: his bike was a heavy roadster with twenty-eight inch wheels, fit for a policeman. 'You had better get your breath back,' I said, 'and then we will get started.'

The flying bedstead.

I pushed my cheese and pickle sandwich deep into my pocket and set off at a brisk pace. We arrived at Cross Hill, which is on the way between Codnor and Heanor. On the road were hundreds of feathers – somehow chickens had got free of their shed and sauntered across the road into the path of a young man on a BSA 500cc Gold Star motorcycle. We at once stopped, helped up the man to his feet and then lifted up the motorcycle: apart from a few scratches to man and machine, everything looked okay.

Not hanging about for the farmer, we set off again in the direction of Heanor. The climb up the hill left us gasping for air as we passed Morley's factory on the right and the Empire cinema on the left. Many's the time my elder sister would take my trousers to work at Morley's to do the turn-up for me, as I had just gone into my first long trousers: twenty-four-inch bottoms were the thing as I got older.

Going downhill was difficult, as the pedals on a fixed wheel never stop turning, and as we approached the MGO garage at Langley Mill I was pouring with sweat. Raymond eased by me and then stopped. 'Hang on,' he said, 'that's enough for now. Let's have a fag', on which he produced a Woodbine paper packet with five cigarettes in it. Any snooker hall or pub had a machine that dispensed cigarettes, which cost no more than ten pence in old money. Today, after thirty-five years underground, a Woodbine would kill me: my lungs are shattered with coal and stone dust.

The road to the hilltop was busy with moving traffic, the smell of new-baked bread, and the clang of a bell as a black Wolsey police car rushed by in the direction of Mellor's pit (Moorgreen Colliery), the poacher/woodsman in the novel *Lady Chatterley's Lover*. We passed the cottage in a row of houses where D.H. Lawrence, the author, once lived. Many, many years later I was to be employed at Moorgreen Colliery.

The road more or less ran through the pit yard, stacks of pit props ready to go underground. There were huge puddles in the road and it wasn't long before Raymond got a puncture.

Alas, we had no puncture-repair kit, so I had a brain wave: going to the verge, we filled the rear tyre with grass. The thing was to pack the grass in as tight as possible in order to take the weight of the rider. We eventually got off the busy main road and looked for directions to Hucknall.

Rolls Royce I knew was at Hucknall: the town supported an aerodrome, nothing like Heathrow of course, but my intuition led me to believe something was going on, thus the bike ride. The great pity was that we hadn't taken a camera with us, as there before our very eyes in the middle of the field was the flying bedstead. No one – and I mean no one – was supposed to know of the tests taking place. Top secret, but there was Staley's lad and his friend Raymond looking at England's secret weapon. If only German intelligence knew about it they might possibly have won the war. Later on, of course, Prince Andrew flew this very plane in the Falklands. It was amazing to see this contraption going up and down only 2ft off the ground.

We had another Woodbine and decided to have our sandwiches before the airforce and the police arrived. I didn't fancy trying to explain to my mother the goings-on at Hucknall field. On returning home, still with grass in Raymond's tyre, I looked forward to a hot bath and an early night. This, as all the other stories are, is true.

Milking Time

I grew up in the small village of Waingroves; three public houses, two shops, both small but which sold almost everything, and a Co-op which almost everyone traded at in order to get the 'divi'. The 'divi' was a means of saving to help out, such as a day trip to Skegness or Blackpool.

It was a glorious morning as I lay in bed, the sun streaming in through the bedroom window and in the corner a spider's web my mother had missed many times through wanting new spectacles which we couldn't afford. I pushed back the bedding; my pillow was so hard it left marks in my neck, and my cover was an old army coat that I'm sure had seen many battles. Within a matter of a few minutes I was dressed and down the stairs. No school today: today was a bank holiday and I meant to make the most of it. A slice of homemade bread and jam and a cup of tea and I was ready to create havoc in the village once more.

Everyone in the village knew 'Staley's lad': I will be the first to admit that I was a little devil, eight years of energy just bursting to get free. The door slammed shut groaning on hinges covered in coats of paint and I was on my way. By 10 a.m. the sun was getting quite warm and the tar-covered pavement was beginning to stick to the soles of my shoes. Woe betide me if I didn't scrape it off before I ventured indoors again!

The road was empty apart from Mr Musson and his GPO red bike. A lovely man, aged about fifty-six years, a stoop in his walk as he delivered the mail, his glasses perched on the end of his nose, with a constant sniffle. Mr Musson tried to avoid me like the plague, although many times he chased me for mimicking him! Anyway, it was a glorious morning, next-door's front garden had daffodils and lilies of the valley in full bloom and the Staffordshire bull terrier had left his calling card.

I crossed to the other side of the road, right in front of the 'beer off' where many times I had stolen a toffee from the counter, the sweets being in open boxes, very tempting for little boys. About fifty yards further on was Abbott's shop as it was known, a shop on the junction of the Main Street and Pit Lane. Next door to the shop was the farm on Pit Lane, and it was time for Walter to go and bring in the dairy cows for milking.

I watched Walter go across the road, down a short way to the gate into the field. The herd of cows was impatient, crowding around the gate and bellowing a sound I can so well remember today, sixty-eight years on. Their bodies seemed to be steaming, and all of them had wet, runny noses. The gate was flung open and there was a mad rush to be first in the sheds for milking.

The road was empty apart from a terrier puppy yapping at the cows' heels as they crossed over. Walter was busy with his stick, poking and prodding to keep the cows out of residents' front gardens. Eventually the road was clear; I say clear, apart from the cowpats steaming across the surface of the road.

I looked up and down the road: it was deserted apart from Mr Musson's cycle, which was propped against the wall next to the letter box. In that instant the devil in me took over. 'Now's my chance,' I thought: I found a stick near the bike and proceeded to fill the letter box with the cow's droppings. As I lifted the stick, I got it all over my clothes, my socks and shoes: I was plastered good and proper. It was when the letter box was full that Staley's lad suddenly realised just what he had done. The smell was terrible: I had even got it in my hair. Mother was waiting for me as I raced to the back door. She looked, and looked again and burst out laughing at me and then, on being told by the postman what the village demon had done, she sobbed bucketfuls. Mr Musson was going hysterical – I had ruined her majesty's mail. The postman was going to inform the police, and by the time PC Plod had arrived I was bathed and shining like a new pin. The outcome of Staley's little terror is to be told in a later story. By the way, all my misfortunes are true and to this day I feel so sorry for my mother, God bless her, and Mr Musson the village postman. I plead guilty.

Wash Day at No. 173: The Follow On

Following the police enquiry over the mail-box episode, and having received the hiding of a lifetime, my bottom unable to bear my weight for a week, I retired to the back garden, a collier's garden, content to do a bit of weeding in order to keep on the right side of my dad.

Ours was a small cottage, two up and two down, semi-detached, a couple of lovely old ladies next door. My grandmother, one of Labour's stalwarts, owned the cottage. Mother kept the cottage spotless, that is to say, following after me. Downstairs, the wallpaper was rather old, some of it starting to unroll at the seams. There was gas lighting, electricity unheard of at this time, just before the outbreak of war in 1939. Our kitchen was a nightmare, no hot water as we have it today, only one brass tap placed over an old stone sink which was yellow with age. The fireplace was a black-leaded, wrought-iron affair with no back boiler. To have a wash was a nightmare, carting ladles full of hot water from the living room into the kitchen.

Outside, hung on a 'dog nail' – that is, a nail from the nearby colliery for fastening down the nails on which the tubs run – was a zinc bath. Many's the time I was bathed in front of the fire in this old tin bath, the carpet a rug pegged from old coats and other scraps of clothing: nothing was wasted, and we all had a go at pegging the rug.

Of all the days in the week, Monday was washday. It was unheard of in Derbyshire to wash on any other day than Monday. To start washday, we had to light the sticks and paper under the cast-iron copper that was built into the brickwork in the corner near the door. Anyone coming to our back door on a Monday would think the house was on fire. Great clouds of steam and smoke from the fire under the copper would be pushing out onto a back yard alive with caterpillars. Near to the door were both cabbages and brussel sprouts. The butterflies had been busy and the garden was full of movement, a mass of caterpillars.

Mother had been up since 7 a.m., changed and made the beds and was now down the garden putting out the clothesline. It was a long garden, going down to the fields with a herd of cows in it. The cows had just returned from milking and I began to think of the punishment I had received the day or so before. I was in the kitchen looking down at the clothesbasket full of mother's washing. No one, and I mean no one, could wash like mother.

Grandma Cope, my mother (left), Auntie Eva (centre) and Uncle Ted (right).

Above: Uncle Ted Cope on my Matchless 500cc with my daughter, Jayne.

Opposite above: Bottom pub, Waingroves.

Opposite below: Jitty for the cows to get to the fields, Waingroves.

Pathway to Waingroves from Wright Avenue.

Ripley pit – the path to Waingroves.

Suddenly, without any thought of my mother whom I loved most dearly, I grabbed the basket, ran to the black-leaded fireplace and stuffed all mother's hard-worked on washing up the chimney. It was nearly ready for sweeping as grandad hadn't swept it lately and so the kitchen filled with soot: everywhere was covered in a blanket of soot. My eyes were burning as every movement made things worse. How could a little boy of such tender years create such mayhem? Mother came running in from down the garden, and in that instant I knew she was heartbroken! With the knowledge of what I had done, I just stood waiting for whatever was to become of me.

Whatever devil was in me left me, I'm pleased to say, and the years have been very kind to me, but often I sit and think of the torment my mother must have been in: with one breath she wanted to strangle me, and the next only a mother's love could forgive me. I thank God my family have the same spirit as that little boy, but manage to control their emotions.

Hands Across the Sea

Today I have attended the funeral of one of the Polish gentlemen who came over to this country in 1947-48 from their native land to help fight against the German army. I have been privileged to work with many of them in collieries in Derbyshire and Nottinghamshire, men who left their country as boys to join our fight as men in all of his majesty's forces. This country of ours owes a debt of gratitude for the bravery these men showed against all odds. Today, as I sit and think of the many friends I have made both at home and at work, I thank God they came to help in our time of need.

I knew if ever there was a pit disaster they would never leave me. It was with a very heavy heart that I said goodbye to one of these Polish gentlemen. These men would take on the worst, the heaviest job with a smile, free to hold their head up high in a foreign land that had taken them in.

My wife and I were invited quite a few times to a Polish club in Nottingham. Their generosity was marvellous; to be made really welcome was wonderful. To see the men, women and children was something to remember, the costumes, the traditional dress with all the different colours was wonderful. To see them dance was great; often we would be invited to join in.

There is one man, a friend for life, Marion is his name; while we worked together he would describe to me his home, a farm on the German/Polish border. Life as a young boy was hard, but when the enemy arrived, they set up guns to fire at English bombers. As he got older Marion was forced to help operate the guns. Today that man has taken up religion to try to atone for things forced on him. From time to time we get a visit from Marion, and it's hard to think that at some time in his life he was shooting down our airmen, but he still has to live with what they forced him to do.

There are many of my questions he cannot or will not answer, but I, as a true friend, will never press him. Most people won't be able to fully comprehend what it's like to lose your home, your family and your country.

My wife and I were introduced to 'Wisniowka,' a drink similar to cherry brandy, though since joining the Salvation Army we neither drink nor smoke. To end my short story, I say, 'good on yer': I take my hat off to you and your present-day families, may you live long and prosper. (4 April 2007)

Above: In uniform – 22405071 PTE Staley, 1950-52.

Opposite above: In remembrance: Waingrove's pit shaft, 1923.

Opposite below: My Methodist chapel, village centre.

Above: Mum and dad's 'middle' pub.

Below: The entrance to Pit Lane.

Above: Ormonde Colliery.

Below: The Jolly Colliers, also known as 'top pub', opposite the Co-op.

Left: My Uncle Eric (circled), miner and dog breeder.

Opposite: Eric's boxing licence.

Seconds Out

As a little boy I was introduced to boxing. My dad used to listen to all the big fights on the wireless: we would sit around the set, a cup of tea on the go every ten minutes, mother grumbling about the washing up and threatening us if we spilt any tea on the sofa.

Saturday night was fight night – Cassius Clay, Gus Lesnavitch, Bruce Woodkock, Brian London, all heavyweights, no one, 'on the fear of death!', should knock at the door while the fight was on. No television then – you had to listen to a commentary, someone who knew a thing or two about boxing. In the early years I remember it was Tommy Farr, a heavyweight who fought for the world title; not very tall, but possessing the heart and strength of a lion.

About the time I started work on the coalface, my Uncle Eric Grainger was ready for hanging up his gloves. A big man, a heavyweight of course, but only part-time as he worked in the afternoons packing and drawing off on the coalface after we had taken away the coal on the day shift. Eric also showed wire-haired terriers and bred them for sale.

On many Sunday mornings I had been going to grandma's but I would call and watch my Uncle Eric wash the dogs, dry and powder them with chalk instead, and the brown saddle would be coffee-stained: whether that was allowed in the show ring I'll never know. Often he would train in the field at the bottom of our garden, the Home Guard keeping their distance. To upset Eric Grainger was playing with fire.

When the fair arrived, Eric would make straight for the boxing booth. The fairground people got to know Eric because he cost them money. The challenge would be thrown out to all comers; anyone to go three rounds with their man would be the winner of the purse. Not many of their boxers lasted three rounds, so I'm sure they were glad to see the back of Eric.

One year the fair was allowed on the football ground instead of the market. The big tent was put up and the boxing ring erected. Outside was a smaller tent with a table inside. My dad took me inside and there was Uncle Eric on the table with his shorts on.

'Les,' he said to my dad, 'get some money out of my trouser pocket and send Keith to Bournes' beer off! Tha knows what I want.' 'I know,' said dad, and sent me off for a pint of whisky. The brand didn't matter, as when I got back Eric took one swig of the bottle – and the rest he got dad to rub all over his body.

Eric's skin was just like leather I imagine to soak up all that punishment; for a miner and part-time boxer he was very good. I remember he fought the contender for Dick Turpin's title after a shift down the pit. Today Eric Grainger has a memorial in Marlpool Cemetery; the likes of Eric I don't think will ever be seen again. God bless him.

Licence N_o 16 990

Valid up to and including

the N A D

s B.B.C.M

1. Record 60 fights Lost 8
   manager Charles Coates
1935   New Inn Sutton in
       Ashfield
took Howard Powell 10 R
3 times. Howard beat Dave
maclean 8 R maclean beat
E. Roderick. Bwa Nick Miller
Zennis Ryan Dennis Buckley
Tommy Martin Deptford
Tiger J Bland J Bramley
Bob Barlow Luther Walker
alf fieldons Lester Terry
Key Frank NewBould
Jim Briardy J Donnelly
Tiger Smith Herbert
Beath J Warren took
Dick Turpin 10 at Leman St
J St Ruments Rejners in 5/10 2/-
E Grainger

Above: Boxing pals and friends.

Opposite: Uncle Eric's boxing record.

Silver Rain

It was a glorious summer's morning as I lay sprawled out on my bed, a shaft of sunlight piercing the corner windowpane, almost setting fire to the faded wallpaper. I could hear the letter box rattle as the paperboy pushed the *Daily Herald* through on to the pegged carpet. There was no rush, I thought, as I put my feet to the floor, catching the 'guzunder' a blow with my feet, a blue and white flowered 'guzunder' bought cheap.

The smell of bacon drifted up the stairs, the stairs waiting to have the carpet renewed, bearing in mind there was no lottery in the 1940s, but only the Littlewoods' football coupons to hope and pray you would get eight draws on.

At this particular time, war was on everyone's mind: the Home Guard had their brush handles and the ARP had their tin hats and torches. Hitler must have been terrified: just imagine, a brush handle against a machine gun, a hand grenade thrown against 'King Edward's potatoes'.

After my bacon butty, the Co-op brown sauce all round my mouth, I put on an old pair of my dad's slippers and made for the back door. Pulling my dressing gown round me, I stepped out into bright sunlight. The sound of Rolls-Royce aero-engines made me immediately look skywards: coming towards our street were four or five Lancaster bombers, I guess at about 600ft. Within a couple of minutes the sky was filled with strips of silver paper. A few moments later a Wolsley police car arrived, the officers telling us not to be alarmed but to gather up the silver paper.

A Lancaster bomber.

Sometime later, word got round on the local grapevine that it was all to do with upsetting the German radar while our planes were over Holland and Germany. Because we lived in Derbyshire, it was difficult to keep anything a secret! We were informed the Lancaster bombers would be making regular runs from Scampton to Lady Bower Dam. Of course, at the time we had no idea what was going off, but they continued low-level flying for some time.

Barnes Wallis, the inventor of the bouncing bomb, lived in our town of Ripley at Butterley Hill. A genius, he also designed the Wellington Bomber, a twin-engined body of wood and canvas. The year was 1943 and to everyone's amazement, the morning papers were full of the raid on the German dams. The Mohne, the Eder, the Sorpe dams all had been breached by Barnes Wallises' bouncing bomb. Many Russian prisoners of war who were living at the base of one of the dams died, but their sacrifice helped to bring the war to an end.

That night nineteen Lancasters took off; eleven returned, battered but with pride in their achievement. To this day at Woodhall Spar there is a memorial to those airmen who undertook practice runs at Lady Bower Dam in Derbyshire. We must never forget Guy Gibson, his crew, his comrades that didn't get back, and of course his beloved pet dog, the faithful black Labrador that was always at his side. At a memorial service it was said that a black Labrador was seen in attendance, but of course he was dead, run over at the camp gates.

I am, as a member of the Salvation Army, proud to know our retired Major Jennings, as during the war she stood on the tarmac to watch 'her boys' go off on night flights, never to return. In the early hours she would be waiting, counting on their return. As Winston Churchill said, 'never in the field of human conflict have we owed so much.' I was a little boy, but I know now they died for me and for England.

Remembrance Day, November 14 1982

She stood alone, in a sea of faces,
Her thoughts were of him, of distant places,
A tear on the cheek, drops to the ground,
The land he died for, where graves abound.

God bless and keep him, not just today,
His charm, his smile, will forever stay,
This hallowed ground, on which she stands,
Flags of all nations, massed brass bands.
He fought and died that she might live,
No greater price could one man give,
They shared this love, but to war he went,
'Love conquers all', it's heaven sent.

Forty years have passed, goodbye's were said,
Now, she stands by his side, as the day they wed,
My heart reaches out, to Max and his wife,
God bless and keep them, I pray for their eternal life.
Love Conquers All.

Share My Life

Get off my back,
Leave me be,
Got to be up,
Bow't half past three

Time for work,
'Who darn well cares?'
Turn back the sheet
Plod down the stairs.

Blowers gone,
Can't be late,
Pit clothes on,
Travel the gate.
Snap times come,
Deputy's been,
Knock-off soon,
Bathed and clean.

Mother's waiting,
Dinner's hot,
Beat dad home,
Scoffed the lot.

Metamorphosis of the Bottle

Neon sign and the bright sky
Dim the windows as the pub runs dry,
'Dry to Him'
Metamorphosis of the bottle.

Lurch the step to door and escape,
'Escape' the bottle, black and tan,
The night of shadows and face of ghosts
Tight the tie, and tight the man,
To drive the cat of black,
'Of course he can.'

Bonnet long, of black and chrome,
Purr the jaguar, travelling home,
A mean machine, a key to start,
A man of drink, and driven hard.

Blurred the eye, and slurred of speech,
Toe the clutch, and crash the gears,
Dead of bottle, grief and tears,
And so the roar as pistons thrash,
Humanity and metal dissolve,
'An instant flash!'

The oak of many suns and moons,
Of wood to cry, as man of human and machine,
Rip asunder the green and brown,
'of colours,'
Colours bathed in blood and multigrade
Black Jags, given birth of engineers.
Oh the waste of three lives gone,
Man, as autumn leaves of oak,

No more to dispatch acorns or seed,
'Today or any day,'
A jaguar of steel and heart,
Inserted by man, torn apart.

Death in View

And there I stood, on wooded knoll,
Eyes of hawk, glint into open grave,
Friends of his, and of mine, their shadows entwine,
Brown the leaf, spiral on wood and brass,
The dead of him, and wet the wood,

Tears of pearls cascade to screw and lid,
Songs on wind, the Welsh lament,
Yellow the daff, and blind the sun,
A host and one, and there I stood,
Farewell, begone old friend,
The golden harp whispers welcome David,
How sweet his name, parchment to scroll,
David the Brave, magnificent in death,
I knew him well,
They call him David, and I respond!

A Notts and Derbyshire Miner!

I awoke to sodden sheets of Irish linen,
The sweat of dreams, of coalface wet,
Seams of black, thick and thin,
'Sometimes hidden',
There I lay, as in the seam, and yet,
The bedroom ceiling was my roof supported,
My walls, the timber of a pinewood forest,
Height of my bed, the height of seam reported, I swear never again, 'the slog',
To be the best.

The Cricket Match

Umpire indicates maiden over.
Eye of age, brain reflects time lost.
Long Grass, cuckoo spit, and maiden fair.
Teenage lass of giggling mouth and so,

And so the team of white on white,
Boot and spikes and rutted green,
Youth bob in grass to spy the day.
Unseen pair, long lost in play
Flat long the grass and green beware.
Gone my youth, my silvers shine the head.
Kiddies suck ice of cone, blow winds of east,
'He's out!', the shout of men in white,
Red the round leather to the three.

They lie till dusk, wicket drawn to time,
Lollipop papers rustle on short and brown,
Brown the locks. Sweated to breast divine,
Giggles lost, so the noon, swathed of moon,
Embrace the last, as ball in flight.

Naked to eye, long gone a voice,
'It's a bye'.

Sweat, Pride and Hellfire

The huge wheels turn, 14ft, to be precise,
Straddled across a pyramid of steel,
White, with snow and ice.

Coal burns, steam hisses, pistons push,
The engine snorts, in its mad rush,

Silver and gold, green and black,
Shining radiant, polished,
With sweated brow, and oily rag.

Onward, ever onward, into the depths below,
The rumble of the chairs, as they pass, to and fro.

This magnificent beast, roaring full throttle,
Sweet cold tea, drunk from a beer bottle.

Clang goes the shovel, as the boilers gulp
In the coal,
Backs ache, in this 'god-forsaken' fire hole.

The fires of Hell, I know of nothing worse,
Stripped naked, to the waist, men spit and curse.

We curse the day that we signed on,
But a job's a job, when said and done.

There's no shame, only pride in what we do,
To have a job, and see it through.

Brother of Mine

The year was 1942 and we were at war. I was ten years of age, not quite understanding the tragic events that were to unfold. We lived in a street which had been purpose-built by the council to house workers for the colliery which was situated at the bottom of our street.

Dad was employed at the colliery along with his father and brother. They were the cream of their trade, employed by Butterley Co. as boilersmiths. This world-renowned firm relied on our family to maintain their colliery boilers. Although the firm thought very highly of my grandfather and his two sons, the pay was terrible.

I was only a child at this particular time, and although dad never took time off work, I could sense something was amiss. Early every morning dad would set off for work, shouting to me as he dropped the latch on the back door, 'Come on, me lad! Let's have you up and see if your mother wants a cup of tea.' Dad knew he could rely on me as I was off school myself. Most children of my age would have loved all this time away from school, forced on me.

The 5.00 a.m. blower would scream out its message to the day shift of men and boys – boys fourteen years of age, setting off to one more day of pitch darkness in the bowels of the earth, with perhaps a carrot or an apple for their favourite pony.

The door banged shut, dad was gone and I eased myself out of bed. I was lucky, the house being semi-detached, and having three bedrooms, the small one mine. Getting dressed was no problem, except that I disliked soap and water, especially round my neck.

I slid down the stairs on my bottom. 'You're there again, you young devil,' mother shouted. 'Sorry, mum,' I replied, and made my way into the kitchen. I knew what to expect on putting on the electric light (and by the way, this was a novelty, as I was so used to lighting the gas). The kitchen wall was a moving mass of broken, dark brown blotches, and as the light was switched on, this moving mass of unhygienic filth would scurry away behind the wall cupboards and the skirting boards, through a space between it and the red-tiled floor which I swear was left by the builders to accommodate those huge beetles.

No one, but no one in the street would admit to the fact that every house had this plague, this infestation of cockroaches. Even the council denied the obvious, but the queue at the town hall for DDT powder exposed the unbearable situation. I made mother a cup of Co-op tea, no sugar, with just a spot of milk, and set off up the stairs. There were twenty-two steps, covered in dark red carpet. I knew from experience there were twenty-two, the bruises on my bottom pleaded guilty. On approaching the bedroom door I could hear my mother softly moaning. I had known for some time that she was ill, but all I got on asking was, 'Little boys should be seen and not heard.'

The tea was hot and had spilled into the saucer. I went into the bedroom, which had emulsion-painted walls because we couldn't afford wallpaper, and pegged rugs covered the floor. Not a cheerful room at all, the curtained window looking out onto steel headstocks of Butterley Co. Mother was very restless, the candlewick bedspread askew, hanging to the floor. Her eyes were sunken and dark. I could see the tears of pain trickling down a white face onto a nightgown of pink cotton with rosebuds embroidered around the neckline.

'I don't want that,' she said. 'What's the time?' 'Dad said you have got to keep taking drinks,' I said. Mother heaved a huge sigh and told me, 'Very shortly your grandmother will be here. I'll try a drink of tea then.' The morning was drizzly, the fine rain seeming so much wetter than if there had been a heavy downpour. I heard the back door go. 'Just a minute,' I said, grandma not knowing the latch was on.

This small, frail woman greeted me at the door, shaking her brolly on entering the kitchen. 'How's your mother?' she said, taking out an enormous hat pin from a large hat that had seen many funerals, its feather bedraggled and limp, looking for a warm fire to straighten it up once more.

Grandma placed her hat and coat near the fire, a collier's fire, stacked halfway up the chimney, a roaring red mass of burning coal, and made her way to the stairs. 'Now then,' she said, looking at me with all the love that a grandmother can show. 'You stop here and let the doctor in.'

'What's he got to come for?' I asked. 'I'm looking after mother.' 'Do as you are told, and don't ask silly questions,' grandmother said, and with a smile for me, gently eased her way up the stairs.

I stood at the bottom of the stairs, and being an inquisitive boy, I tried to listen to the snatches of conversation. 'He's not at school again,' I heard grandma say. Being school governor, she was the one I turned to when I was in trouble over bad attendance. I loved her deeply, perhaps more than my own mother and father.

A loud knock at the door startled me. Only a policeman or a doctor would use the front door, which groaned at being opened, paint joining together every hinge. I turned the key and pulled back the bolts, top and bottom of the door refusing to break the paint covering the hinges.

I forced the door open as best a boy of ten slender years could and there stood Dr Ryan, a large man, well-made but with a stoop. His dark overcoat shone at the collar and cuffs. Dr Ryan was a man of the people, not one for airs and graces.

One didn't have to know his name to see he was Irish through and through. His face gave him away: the blarney shone through the rain, a rain drop hanging from his large nose and his thin silver hair crying out for a warm towel.

Outside was his pride and joy, a Rover two-door tourer. It was a magnificent car by any standards, with the black and chrome still as new and a thick off-white canvas hood, with brackets in the style of a Silver Cross pram. The tyres were white-walled tyres of Dunlop manufacture set on steel chromed wheels.

Many's the time I've filled the boot of that wondrous car with coal from a well-stocked coal house. 'Good morning, doctor, won't you come in?' The old gentleman entered into the hallway, wiping his feet on a cocoa-matting square, the ends of which were beginning to fray.

I led him to the bottom of the staircase and shouted to grandmother who had never left my mother's side. 'Morning, doctor,' she said and let him in, closing the bedroom door to shut me out, not knowing the significance of what was about to change my whole life.

I sat poking the fire listening to horrible screams from upstairs. By the time the doctor came down, what had been a roaring fire was merely a glow. Dr Ryan looked very sad. Something bad had taken place in my mother's bedroom, and I knew I mustn't ask.

There was the sound from the kitchen of soap passing from hand to hand, the rumble of water as it replaced water used from the hot water tank. The doctor came in and let himself out of the front door, not uttering one word. My love for that old man, who ten years earlier had brought me into the world, knew no bounds. I will love that old Irish doctor till the day I die.

I heard the engine cough, and then roar into life. He was gone! Not knowing what to expect, I sat poking the dying embers once again, little realising a dying fire was to bring thoughts of death and the dying. There was a soft gentle voice calling me: grandma was at the top of the stairs. 'Mend the fire,' she said. 'I want you.' What was to happen next changed a boy of ten into a man.

'I want you to be very brave,' grandma said, hugging me to her. Whatever could she mean? I hadn't done anything wrong I was sure. She took my hand and led me into the bedroom. A funny smell, a hospital smell, filled my nose as we entered the room.

Mother was fast asleep, or so I thought. A pile of bedding sat in one corner of the room; I noticed it was stained bright red. There was no movement from my mother, not so much as a pulse from the bedding to indicate she was breathing. I was led by a tight grandmother's hand to the opposite side of the double bed. A baby's cot caught my eye. Something very strange was happening.

Grandma stooped down, arms going towards what I thought was some more washing. Straightening up, she gently moved aside the white cotton sheet. There before me was a baby! The most beautiful baby ever. It was a silent baby. Not so much as a whimper. Tiny spots of blood stood out on the baby's forehead. Spots of blood on the eyelids and on its tiny fingers.

'What is it?' I asked. 'Why doesn't it cry?' grandma said, 'You have a baby brother.' 'What's wrong? Why doesn't he move?' I asked.

'He's gone to Jesus in the sky,' she said, trembling with emotion, the feelings tearing at her frail body. 'Why has he gone to Jesus?' I asked. At Sunday school we are told Jesus loves little children. I cried and cried, tears enough to put out the fire roaring away downstairs.

Long after that tearful day, I found out where he was buried. (Not even a name.) Grandma took me to his grave. There was no marker for my brother, just a mound of new-turned earth and a grass sod in a hedge bottom. Fifty years on I still know the spot, emblazoned in my heart and mind for all eternity.

A Vellocette Venom, and Paris in the Spring

The year was 1956, spring was in the air, and I was a young man who wanted to take on the world. The pit yard was a million miles away as I started my brand-new Vellocette Venom 500cc, and as it roared into life, I made for Nottingham, the RAC office, with the intention off getting over the channel come hell or high water. In a matter of half an hour, the booking was made, two berths on the channel steamer, plus a space for my motorcycle. The extra berth was for my cousin Ivor, a young man who spent all his leisure time trying to quench an almighty thirst with Mansfield Bitter.

Earlier in the week, I had approached Ivor with the idea of going off to France, and he seemed intrigued with the thought of setting out on my Vellocette to the land of champagne and. horse meat… I did however stress there would be no Mansfield Bitter once off the boat.

The bike, a 500cc single, was in highly polished chrome and black enamel, and half-hidden under the petrol tank was the engine, made of aluminium, a very powerful engine in those days, fast and light.

Harry Middleton of Ripley, a big racing man at that time, had sold me the bike, and I went along to see if he would fit me some Craven Panniers for carrying all the extra clothing we would need. Harry was a marvellous man, and a brilliant engineer; he had worked for Rolls Royce during the war. 'Come round tomorrow and we'll fix you up,' he said, with his usual smile and a sparkle in his eyes.

The next week or so was taken up arranging passports and money at the bank, the rest of the gear being purchased at the Army & Navy stores. Finally the day arrived for the off, a glorious morning, the sun already warming up the road, mist clinging to the tarmac, penetrated by the sun's rays, and the birds already in full song. I took a great gulp of the morning air: it felt good to be alive. I lifted the haversack with all the cooking utensils inside on to my back. Mum and dad came to see me off, and as I straddled my machine, I'd swear I heard dad say to mum, 'Let's hope he takes his time,' as she knew that I had just been done for speeding.

Those days, it was the in thing to get done for speeding at least twice a year – the papers had a field day when we all appeared at the local magistrates' court. The fine was usually about two pounds, which in those days was quite a lot of money, as wages were very poor in the 1950s.

We were referred to as the Ton-Up Boys, or, as some called us, Café Crawlers, never bothering with 'L' plates; a girl on the pillion and ORF you'd jolly well go! Anyway, the bike was purring like a kitten as I made my way round to Ivor's. I turned the corner of the street and tweaked the throttle, just a touch. The front wheel of the bike reared up as the engine came on full song, simply magic… Barry Sheene was still in his cradle when we were raising hell: Geoff Duke was the lad in our day, John Surtees and Bob McIntyre. I saw them all at different meetings. One up-and-coming local lad, a friend of mine, Monty Buxton, started racing on a 350cc BSA Gold Star and a 500cc later to race Manx Nortons, a bike the world's best riders had at that time.

To get back to the trip… Ivor was all packed and ready, a suitcase and a Co-op carrier bag containing an extra pair of shoes. The case had to be strapped on top of the panniers, leaving room for Ivor to sit on the pillion. Crash helmets were not compulsory all those years ago, a flat cap, back to front, so the blink didn't get in the way of the RAF goggles served the purpose.

Opposite: Mum and dad and my sister Barbara in Skegness, 1938.

Right: Ivor Staley, my cousin, and Ray Stone, both miners.

Mum and dad at Rhyl Miners' Holiday Camp.

A long scarf wrapped around his mouth and across his chest to keep out the wind was Ivor's dress of the day. What a sight we must have looked, as we set off with forty pounds in our back pockets.

Derby was soon behind, the old road in my opinion far better than the motorways of today: the Vello seemed to eat up the miles, only stopping for petrol, and a quick drag on a Woodbine before setting off once more at a steady pace. As the morning traffic began to filter on to the main road, people going to work, the smell of newly-baked bread was in the air, the trolley buses were sparking as the conductor changed the poles from one set of overhead wires to another, and our thoughts were to press on, on to London and Dover.

The signs for the outer London ring road came up – as we gave the bike some throttle to overtake a lorry laden with coal, I shouted to Ivor, clinging on for grim death, 'I bet we got the coal out, the day before'. The lorry had been travelling at a fair speed, causing a vacuum at the rear, and the coal dust was swirling about as the load hadn't been sheeted over.

I felt the dust in my eyes and on my tongue, and decided to pull in at one of the many transport cafés to be seen at the roadside. Shutting off the engine, I pulled off the road, and while Ivor stretched his legs, I made for a grotty looking toilet, the door hanging by the one hinge. On entering, I glanced at a broken mirror over the wash basin. I had a second look – I had a jet black face and two enormous white eyes where the goggles had been! My handkerchief and a parched tongue managed to get rid of most of the dirt, and it wasn't long before I was enjoying a sweet mug of tea, Ivor having a good laugh at my expense.

Out on the forecourt, one or two of the lorry drivers were admiring the Vello: well, it was the first to come into Derbyshire, and I was very proud of the fact. Climbing onboard, we soon were on our way, the telegraph poles whizzing past at an alarming rate, and the weather changing from county to county.

After what seemed an eternity, we were entering the outskirts of Dover, the sea breeze refreshing and a salty tang to the lips. It didn't take long to find the seafront and the harbour and ask the way to the customs. No one bothered us as we made our way to the ship; cars were streaming in from all directions trying to get a good berth onboard. The bike took the climb up the long winding slope into the ship's hold in its stride, changing down the gears to almost a crawl. 'Well, we've arrived,' I said, pushing out the prop stand to rest the bike, 'let's go and find our cabin'.

Cabin thirteen was our berth, but at that moment I couldn't have cared less – off with the heavy Barbour suit and the Wellingtons, (I couldn't afford proper boots), and on to the bunk bed. Ivor wanted to toss a coin to see who had top bunk, but it was too late, I was shattered after the long drive down. The ship's blower wailed out and we were off.

A prod in the ribs brought me back to the land of the living, Ivor was standing over me pointing to the porthole, with a surprised look on his face. 'Come on!' he said, waving his arms about, 'look at this lot.' The sight was something I will never forget – sunken ships, their masts protruding from a calm sea, throwing long shadows across the water and giving one a very queer feeling in one's gut. A seagull rested on one of the high masts, catching its breath before venturing on, and as I watched the masts gently tilting to and fro, the sea swilling in and out of their sunken bodies, my thoughts were of 1940, and British Army fast on the beaches, trying to escape the bullets and bombs of the invading army. Planes diving into the sea, riddled with tracer bullets, a parachute in the sky, the pilot slumped in his harness. I retreated to the bunk as a moment of sadness crept over me.

The next thing I remember was a ship's blower sounding as we were about to enter Dunkirk harbour. Ivor and I collected our belongings and made our way on deck, the harbour was alive, people jostling to get off the ship, cars and buses cramming the narrow streets and horse-drawn carriages waiting for customers. We had arrived.

On disembarking, we had to go through customs, a mere formality as it's only on entering Dover again that anyone pays you any attention. Passports were checked, the bike given a quick look over and we were on our way. Paris, here we come!

I kicked up the bike and we were on our way, the sun on our backs, and not a care in the world. We had no sooner set off than I had to do an emergency stop: I heard the noise of a continental hooter blaring out, and suddenly realised that we were on the wrong side of the road! The driver of the bus was furious, his arms up in the air waving frantically. There was little time to use hanging about here, I thought, give the bike some power and get the heck out of it. The big Vellocette roared to life and we shot off, not even daring a backward glance at the uproar I had caused.

Once out on to the open road, away from the cobblestones, we were amazed at the long rows of tall poplar trees, 60, 70, 80ft tall on either side of the road, they reached up to the heavens, massive and majestic, a sight to behold. I remember seeing those trees on the Pathé News as a child, as the German armoured divisions poured into the coastal towns; the fact is, what you see and hear as a child stays with you.

Pushing on, but ready for a break, I noticed a derelict farm house standing back amongst the trees, so I slowed down and Ivor and I strolled over to investigate. There was a gaping hole in the roof, and the door was hanging off; I wouldn't have thought any one was living there. We approached with caution, and entered the building. The farm house consisted of three rooms, a living room, a kitchen, and a small bedroom. To tell the truth, I had visions of a large German soldier waiting at the back of the door. I held back. Ivor, taking the initiative, stepped forward. 'Come on,' he said, 'stop messing about, let's mash.' (The term means to make tea.)

The kettle soon came to the boil – a paraffin pressure stove in an old biscuit tin was a very handy thing to have with you when travelling light. Sweet tea sooths the nerves, so I insisted on three heaped teaspoons; a quick drag on a Woodbine, and we had a gander (a quick look). On the floor in the bedroom were 303 bullet cartridges; we picked some up to save for when we arrived back home. 'Just think', I said, 'this place could tell a tale or two.'

The weather began to deteriorate as we mounted the bike and set off once more, the sun had disappeared behind some clouds and it had started to rain, wet rain, the sort of rain that soaks you through in seconds. In the distance I could see a bridge, one made of wood, with a canopy over, just like in the films. We took shelter till the shower had passed, and then continued with journey.

It must have been well into the afternoon as we entered the outskirts of Paris. It's funny, you know, neither of us had a clue how to communicate with the residents. How does one say 'bed and breakfast' in French? In the distance we could see the Eiffel Tower and we headed in that direction: only a fool could get lost, I thought. Not five minutes later we were trying to make two young ladies understand exactly what we required. Please believe me, I only asked the way, but was given a huge smile and Ivor was beckoned over. Then the penny dropped.

'Get on that bike – quick!' I shouted to Ivor, the colour rising in my cheeks. 'Let's get moving before we get arrested!' 'What's up youth?' Ivor said. The broad Derbyshire accent came across once again; 'what's yer hurry?' Never mind, just get on the bike and let's go, the ladies laughing at our quick departure.

You know, to this day I'm not sure which way to go round a Parisian roundabout – we were really green when it came to holidays but here we were, two colliers with forty pounds apiece and no bed for the night.

The large green and white road sign indicated we were on the Champs Elysées, and so I headed the bike towards the Arc de Triomphe, moving in and out of the heavy traffic, motorists quite oblivious, it seemed, to one another. Ivor indicated that he must pay a call to nature, and observing the traffic, I pulled onto the roadside. The assorted shops and cafés were doing a brisk trade as we wandered up and down the wide pavement looking for a gentleman's toilet. There appeared to be a large wrought-iron grid just to the left of a huge sycamore tree in the middle of the pavement, and we observed men going behind this scruffy screen. Low and behold, this was the toilet, and we went in. If you can imagine standing there, your head and shoulders above this monstrosity, peering over the other side of the street, trying to look inconspicuous as a bus passes by then one will realise the embarrassment we felt. For the first time, I wished I was home.

Time was pressing: we still had to find a room for the night. The Vello gave a cough as I started it up, perhaps an objection to all the stopping and starting since leaving the ship. Various hotels were passed; it was getting late, but I was determined not to take any hotel, and then we saw the sign HOTEL SAINT LOUIS '75, Rue Saint Louis en I'Ile, Paris. DIJOLS, Proprietaire.'

'That's the one,' I said, 'that'll do nicely, let's see if there's any room for us.' The gentleman at the desk made us very welcome, speaking in English, 'put your motorcycle round the back of the hotel and I will show you the room.' The room was quite spacious, a large double bed, made of solid brass, clean as a new pin. 'What about this then,' Ivor said, making a beeline for the bed. The manager left the room, and I promptly jumped on the other side of the bed, heaving a sigh of relief at the thought of not having to spend the night with the down-and-outs of Paris on top of a Metro manhole cover.

Why I tell you this is, we had noticed on our rounds of the hotels these unfortunate people lying on those grate covers and could see the warm air rising from the underground railway system. A type of open-air central heating. We both commented on the appalling conditions those poor people lived in, and how lucky we were in the circumstances.

The hot bath was great: steaming hot water and the pair of us had a long soak in turn. Not surprisingly, it was well after 10 p.m. when we settled down for the night, thinking of the morning and our new adventure.

The sound of traffic woke us. I got out of bed and walked over to the window, opened the catch and pulled the French windows open wide. What a glorious morning! The sun streamed in the room, and as I stepped out on to the balcony I was met with the hustle and bustle of a great city, the chatter of people as they sat taking morning coffee and fresh bread rolls, the church bells ringing out a welcome, and the police man standing on his little rostrum, blowing his whistle and directing the busy traffic. My cousin and I dressed, putting aside the motorcycle gear until it was needed again, and made our way downstairs to partake of the coffee and rolls. The arrangement was that we would stay for two nights, and then move on to another part of the city.

That day Ivor and I took in as many of the sights as our legs would allow: Notre Dame, the Place de la Concorde, the Arc de Triomphe, enjoying every second of it, only stopping when postcards were thrust at us from all directions, dare I say more!

The market traders were in full song as we passed through the open-air market, men scurrying about with apple baskets on their heads, a dozen or more at one go, however they managed to balance them I'll never know. Fish the likes of which I had never seen before hanging up for sale, the heat of the day creating a terrible pemm (smell).

Huge trays of melons and peaches were perched on heads, a cigarette hanging from the corner of the porters' mouths, the black berets and striped jumpers aglow in the sunshine of that lovely day. 'Oh I Remember it Well', the warm night air, the glow of the neon signs, and the music filtering over from a bar.

The sight of the Moulin Rouge hit us from across the street: a multi-coloured windmill over the entrance was twirling away with lights flashing various colours at intervals as we took the bull by the horns (now or never) and stepped inside.

Previous page: Paris.

This page: Wonderful Paris on £40 and Switzerland by Vellocette Venom 500cc; below is the border between France and Switzerland.

The room was large and very dark, apart from the centre, which was floodlit. We sat at a table skirting the edge of the centrepiece, and a waiter came over for our order. Ivor, in his broad Derbyshire accent, said: 'it's muck or nettles lad – what yer 'aving?' 'Champagne!' I replied, to his astonishment. Why not, let's live dangerously. He looked at the wine list and sputtered 'crikey, its five pounds a bottle!' I said, 'Sip it.'

The show commenced and believe me or believe me not, a male and female took the floor: true as I sit here, they hadn't a stitch between them. We looked, we looked again, and then we looked at each other. I had heard men talking down the pit about such things, BUT this was real, here and now.

A smile appeared on Ivor's face, and turned into a grin the size of a banana. I coloured up: I could feel my cheeks begin to burn, and burst out laughing, I just couldn't help myself, not expecting anything like this to happen. Champagne or no champagne, we downed the bottle and beat a hasty retreat to the door. That, I might add, was the first and last time we paid a visit to the famous MOULIN ROUGE.

The following day we met up with some Americans, and it didn't take long before Ivor, the four Americans and I were chatting over a meal on the banks of the river Seine. The river was alive with tourists in rowing boats and motor boats of all shapes and sizes; it was as though everyone had decided to come to the city of l'amour.

The meal was something to remember, marvellous, all and more I should say. It wasn't until we had all got up from the table, and I was remarking on the steak, that Al, one of our American friends, let us into the secret: 'Hey man, that was no steak,' he said, 'that was horse, man! That was a horse.' I looked in the direction of Ivor. 'Don't look at me,' he said, 'mine was alright', and smiled, as if to say, 'What do you expect in France?'

To this day, Ivor ard I sit and talk of the time two young men went to Paris, the friends they made, the sights they saw and that wonderful journey from a mining town in Derbyshire to France and back.

The end of the road: Keith and Ivor, ready for a cup of tea and a woodbine.